# Improving Competitiveness
## of Industry

# Improving Competitiveness of Industry

## of Industry

**Harold Bierman, Jr**

Cornell University, USA

**World Scientific**

NEW JERSEY · LONDON · SINGAPORE · BEIJING · SHANGHAI · HONG KONG · TAIPEI · CHENNAI

*Published by*

World Scientific Publishing Co. Pte. Ltd.

5 Toh Tuck Link, Singapore 596224

*USA office:* 27 Warren Street, Suite 401-402, Hackensack, NJ 07601

*UK office:* 57 Shelton Street, Covent Garden, London WC2H 9HE

**British Library Cataloguing-in-Publication Data**
A catalogue record for this book is available from the British Library.

ISBN-13 978-981-4355-18-6
ISBN-10 981-4355-18-6

Printed in Singapore.

# Preface

As the twenty-first century begins, the world finds itself with a wide range of possible economic futures. Many corporations conclude that it is difficult to compete in international markets with the result being shrinking revenue. Too many governments utilize an excessively high percentage of their nation's goods and services. Bankrupt Greece is buying costly submarines and fighter planes.

In the past, some countries could afford to have a less than perfect tax system. However, wage and other labor rigidities (work rules) handcuff management. Management has become preoccupied with non-productive pursuits, and numerous other sources of inefficiency.

The objective of this book is to suggest several revisions in institutional structure, management techniques and rewards, and a drastic change in how hourly labor is paid. The suggestions offered are applicable to any economy where decisions have to be made as to how to organize the factors of production most efficiently.

I readily concede that the exact initiation of implementation of many of my suggestions will be difficult. However, it is essential that a start be made toward an industrial economic system that is efficient as well as fair.

*Harold Bierman, Jr.*
*Cornell University*
*Ithaca, N.Y.*

# Acknowledgments

My primary facilitator on this project was my support aide and typist, Barbara Drake. She was efficient and reliable and always cheerful.

My son, H. Scott Bierman, helped with a segment of the book. Sy Smidt helped me develop key ideas regarding capital budgeting.

For better or worse, the book is primarily the result of my efforts. I cannot assign blame to others.

*Harold Bierman, Jr.*

# Contents

*Preface*                                                                    v

*Acknowledgments*                                                          vii

Chapter 1    An Agenda for Increasing Productivity:                          1
             An Introduction

Chapter 2    Corporate Tax Modification Proposals                            5

Chapter 3    Productivity and the Net Present Value                         13
             Calculation

Chapter 4    A Managerial Incentive Strategy for Increased                  21
             Productivity

Chapter 5    Economic Income                                                35

Chapter 6    Flexible Wages: A Wage Plan for Increased                      47
             Productivity

Chapter 7    Industrial Democracy                                           59

Chapter 8    Correcting One Problem: Introducing Present                    71
             Value Depreciation

Chapter 9    Using Earnings Per Share and Stock Prices to                   83
             Measure Managerial Performance

Chapter 10   Ten Management Errors                                    89

Chapter 11   Costs of Capital by Division                             97

Chapter 12   Mergers, Acquisitions, and LBOs                         103

Chapter 13   Little Differences and Big Results                      109

Chapter 14   Scientific Management                                   117

Chapter 15   Corporate Strategies                                    121

Chapter 16   Achieving an Improved Competitive Position              125

*Index*                                                              133

# Chapter 1

# An Agenda for Increasing Productivity: An Introduction

All political parties want to increase social welfare. Some of us pay particular attention to how the nation's total product (GNP) is distributed and there is a large amount of interest in the extent of differences in the levels of income and wealth. Others see social progress in terms of a size of a pie and are interested in making a pie grow so that there is more to distribute. Both issues are of importance, but this book is primarily concerned with how to increase the size of the pie, the amount of goods and services available to the population. Distributional issues are always present, but are subordinated in this book to the objective of increasing productivity and total output of the industrial sector.

We start with an assumption that people can be motivated by economic incentives and we should design systems that lead to the actions that society wants. To accuse people of being motivated by self-interest is harsh, but to ignore the importance of self-interest is criminal since implementing policies that ignore self-interest steals from all of us.

Let us first consider the tax system. It is not sensible to want one outcome (increased savings and productivity) and have a tax system that discourages real investment. The present system in many countries also encourages undesirable financial manipulation at the corporate level and distracts management from the essential tasks of developing, designing, producing and marketing of products. Chapter 2 offers a corporate tax reform proposal and suggests an overhaul of the tax system, with less reliance on income taxes.

Another area of improvement is in the corporate managerial sector. I am concerned with how management's performance is measured and how management is rewarded for its efforts. Rewards should be based on performance today and tomorrow.

Consistent with my suggestion on how to reward management, we want to revamp the system used to pay labor. A high labor cost frequently results in labor going idle. I want a "flexi wage" system that offers labor a strong incentive to work, possibly at a lower incremental rate (we would expect the annual wage to be larger) and for management to make decisions that lead to more goods and services.

Another aspect of management where I recommend changes is in the practice of evaluating investments. While most large corporations use some forms of discounted cash flow method, there are deficiencies in their application. The use of excessively high discount rates results in rejecting good increasing efficiency type of investments. A second deficiency is to fail to consider all consequences of rejecting an investment. Also, while most large firms do use a discounted cash flow calculation, many firms still use methods of calculation that cannot be used effectively as the basis of making investment decisions.

Finally, I am concerned with the amount of time and effort (and money) that is spent on merger and acquisition activities that are driven by tax considerations. I would like to eliminate the corporate tax motivation for such activity, but I do not object to merger and acquisition activity that is truly motivated by a desire to increase efficiency. I have faith in the ability of the financial community to evaluate whether or not this type of activity is beneficial for the players initiating the activity, but there is no reason to conclude that private equity raiders are thinking in terms of the effects of their actions on gross national product.

I believe that little differences in the system being employed (tax, wage payments and managerial incentives) have massive effects on productivity through time. People are heavily influenced by the signals (rewards and penalties) that are communicated to them. If these signals are not consistent with increasing productivity, then the economic system will slow, even if it does not change immediately in a dramatic fashion. At any given moment in time, there are many factors affecting productivity. I am only focusing on a selected few, which are relatively easy to modify.

Increases in productivity ultimately occur because of a healthy symbiosis of managers, workers, and capital payment. There is currently taking place a revolution in the types of automated equipment available as the computer revolution proceeds at an increasing pace. I want to insure that systems are in place that will best use the electronic marvels that are available. This book does not describe how to design a new machine that will increase productivity. It does recommend some changes in the economic structures that will enhance the likelihood that we all benefit from the new machines.

If there are imperfections in the present system of allocating and using resources, are there known feasible improvements? Let the debate and thinking begin.

# Chapter 2

# Corporate Tax Modification Proposals

Corporate taxes are relatively efficient vehicles for central governments to use for tax collections. Unfortunately, the method of computing taxable corporate income is flawed (results in undesirable motivations) as is the basic premise that the legal fiction, a corporation, can pay income taxes, thus reducing the taxes that "people" pay.

In some countries, the maximum corporate rate exceeds the maximum personal tax rate. Contrary to popular wisdom, the shift in emphasis from the individual income tax to the corporate income tax will not shift taxes from people to corporations. It is difficult for some people to believe this conclusion, but only people can bear taxes. From a logical point of view, people — stockholders, workers, landlords, consumers, etc. — bear taxes. A corporation cannot. Thus, when a politician declares that "business must pay its fair share of taxes", it is not clear what this means.

It is worthwhile to note that the political appeal of the corporate income tax is most likely due to the fact that the impact of the tax is incredibly well-hidden. Indeed, economists have long debated but have yet resolved the question of which group of people actually pays the corporate income tax. To the extent politicians can convince the public that "business" especially "big business" pays the tax, they have a politically cheap method of collecting taxes. But the fact is that the big corporation does not pay the taxes but rather people pay.

## Capital Structure and Corporate Taxes

The tax laws make an important distinction between earnings on debt and earnings on stock. Earnings on debt is called interest and interest is treated by the issuing corporation as a tax deduction. Thus, with a 0.35 corporate tax rate, $100 of interest paid saves $35 of taxes for a corporation implying a net interest cost of only $65. On the other hand, $100 paid to stock investors has no tax-reducing capabilities and has a net cost of $100. The same situation can be looked at on a before-tax basis. To return $100 after-tax to investors, the corporation must either issue debt and earn $100 before-tax, or issue stock and earn $153.85 before-tax. That is, the corporation must earn 53.85 percent more with stock than with debt to pay the same $100 return on capital.

These considerations have led to theoretical valuation models which quantify the effect on firm value of substituting debt for stock equity. The increased value of the firm associated with substituting debt for equity can be large and has been a strong motivation for mergers, acquisitions of firms, and leveraged buyouts. Furthermore, the substitution of debt for common stock has become a popular defense against unfriendly mergers.

The cost to society of the financial restructuring of corporations has undoubtedly been much larger than the loss of tax revenues. Good investment projects become risky and impossible to finance when the first priorities of the firm become the avoidance of bankruptcy and debt repayment.

A somewhat more subtle but equally important distortion caused by the corporate income tax, concerns the flow of resources between the corporate and noncorporate sectors. The corporate income tax is not a tax on economic profits. Since interest expenses are deductible, the tax base for the corporate income tax includes both economic profits and a normal return on equity capital. The double taxation of stock equity income at the corporate and personal levels means that capital will flow from the highly taxed corporate sector to the lower taxed noncorporate sector or to highly leveraged (debt utilization) corporations. This flow will continue until the after-tax rates of return are equalized across sectors. The importance of this flow is that investment projects with relatively high before-tax returns are foregone in the corporate sector in lieu of investment projects with relatively low before-tax social benefits. Therefore, potentially large distortions in resource usage are generated by tax differences between the corporate and noncorporate sectors.

We will now consider a set of tax modification proposals.

## The Integration of Corporate and Personal Tax Rates

Let us consider a system of taxation whereby corporate income is attributed to the owners of the corporation and investors are taxed as having earned income when the corporation earns income. The proposal to integrate corporate and partnership tax rate has a fairly long history. For a discussion of many of the issues surrounding the debate, see *The National Tax Journal*, March 1975.

To minimize tax evasion, the corporation would withhold and pay a tax on the income it earns, independent of who owns the stock of the firm. The tax paid and withheld would be credited to the investor's tax and would increase the investor's income. If no tax is paid by the investor, there will be a minimum tax on its share of the income earned by the corporation.

If a corporation uses debt and has interest expense, the corporation will withhold a 35 percent tax that can be used as a payment of taxes by the investor subject to tax. With a $100 interest expense, the investor paying a 35 percent tax would report $100 of income and use the $35 withheld by the corporation to pay the tax. The investor would receive $65 cash from the corporation, the same amount as if stock had been used. A zero tax investor receiving the $65 interest payment would pay no tax but the $35 withheld by the corporation would go to the tax collector. Some or all of the $35 could be refunded to the investor. The objective of this provision is to eliminate any tax advantage of debt. Debt interest and common stock returns would be taxed the same.

With corporate income taxed as if earned by the shareholders and with debt not having tax advantages, there are a number of pleasant ramifications. First, there is no tax advantage to the retention of earn-ings versus dividend distribution (but also, no disadvantage). Second, there is no tax induced incentive to reorganize a company or to acquire a firm. Third, the elimination of the tax advantage of interest means that the financing of investment projects through debt has no tax advantage over equity financing. Fourth, corporate income would be taxed at the same rate as noncorporate income, implying that investment capital will flow to projects with the greatest social value.

Zero tax investors could be treated differently depending upon objectives that are considered desirable. An investor that is zero tax because of insufficient earnings could get a tax refund for the amount withheld by the corporation. An investor that is zero tax because of its nature (say a university) could be taxed at a lower rate than the maximum individual tax rate. Foreign investors would be taxed under special tax provisions.[1]

The elimination of double taxation will cost the Treasury some tax revenue but the elimination of the interest deduction will help the Treasury. To maintain revenue neutrality individual tax rates could rise slightly (there are other revenue sources available such as a value-added tax, but an increase in the maximum individual income tax rate seems most likely). Current owners of stock equity facing a marginal tax rate less than 35 percent would benefit from the integration of corporate and partnership tax rates. The post change financial posi-tion of high-tax investors would depend on the maximum marginal tax rate, whether the corporation in which they had invested was retaining earnings or paying a dividend.

## Capital Gains Taxes

A question arises as to how to tax capital gains. One appealing solution is to change the tax basis of an investment by the amount of

---

[1] For a well-thought-out list of the administrative difficulties associated with integra-tion, see McLure, C.E. Jr. (1979). *Must Corporate Income Be Taxed Twice?* The Brookings Institution, Washington, D.C., pp. 146–185.

the corporate income that is subject to tax. Assume an investor pays $10 per share for a stock. If $5 per share is earned before tax and $1.70 of tax is withheld by the corporation, then $5 will be added to the investor's tax basis, which becomes $15. If the shares are sold for $17, the resulting net capital gain of $2 can then be taxed at the statutory rate for capital gains.

The most important benefit from the integration of corporate and personal tax rates is that it will induce firms to base decisions concerning investment projects, mergers, corporate structure, and capital structure on economic variables as opposed to artificially and unintentionally constructed tax incentives.

## Eliminating Interest as a Deduction

An alternative to the integration of corporate and personal tax rates is to retain the corporate income tax but modify the tax base on which it is calculated. I propose that the deduction for interest expense in computing the taxable income of a corporation be eliminated. Interest is simply a return on invested capital in the same way that dividends are a return on invested capital. To allow one type of return on capital (interest) to be a tax shield and another return on capital (dividends) not to be a shield is to distort a rational approach to corporate finance. To keep the tax system revenue neutral, the corporate tax rate could be lowered.

The primary advantage of this reform is that it would eliminate the massive tax incentives for management to use debt to either acquire other firms, or to prevent a raider from acquiring its firm. While corporate takeovers are a useful tool to improve the efficiency of management, excessive debt leverage also changes real investment plans in ways that may not be desirable to society. When a corporation with a normal capital structure prepares a $250 million capital budget, but in response to a raider modifies its plans to form a $100 million capital budget, it is likely that more than fat has been cut from the budget.

I am not objecting to the issuance of debt by a competent management. I am objecting to what amounts to a Federal tax subsidy associated with issuing debt. Today a management might consider a debt-equity ratio of 0.3 to be an optimum capital structure from the viewpoint of the firm accepting a normal amount of operating risk. This same management, faced with a raider, and attempting to realize tax reduction possibilities, might change to a debt-equity ratio of 0.9.

To solve problems arising from sole proprietorship which clearly pay interest to pure debt investors, a maximum amount of interest could be allowed as a tax deduction.

## Leveling the Playing Field

Assume eliminating the debt-interest deduction is not an acceptable alternative. To equalize the pros and cons of debt and equity, common stock could be allowed a tax deduction at the same rate as the debt interest.

But assume that this tax change lowers the tax revenues below the target amount, then the amount of debt interest allowed as a tax deduction could be reduced and the same percentage could be applied to the implicit common stock deduction.

Assume a firm is paying $100,000,000 interest (assume a 5 percent interest rate) but only $60,000,000 is allowed to reduce the corporate taxable income. The 5 percent interest rate would be applied to the common equity but only 60 percent of the 5 percent of the common equity would be allowed as a tax deduction.

There would be many ways of implementing the proposal. The important factor would be reducing the tax deduction for debt interest and increasing the deduction for the interest cost on common stock equity so that the incentives to use debt as part of the tax strategy is reduced.

## The Use of Debt

Corporations use debt for many different reasons. A basic reason is that a corporation needs capital to perform its economic functions. But the capital it needs does not necessarily have to be debt capital.

A corporation uses debt rather than common stock for the following reasons:

a. Does not dilute ownership control.
b. Increases the return on equity if more than the cost of debt is earned on the incremental assets.
c. Adds net after tax cash flow compared to equal cost equity (after tax).
d. Consistent with explanation (c) the use of debt instead of common stock equity adds value to the equity investors because of the debt tax shield.

If $1,000,000 of 0.10 debt is used instead of equity with a 0.35 corporate tax rate, and with the purchased asset having an infinite life, the value added by using debt rather than stock is

$$t \, (\text{Amount of Debt}) = 0.35(\$1,000,000) = \$350,000.$$

This 35 percent of value added is material.

## Conclusions

The objectives of the tax modifications described in this chapter are to eliminate several important distortions which are created by the current corporate income tax laws. Corporations with a modest amount of debt capital will be benefited by these changes.

Eliminating differential taxation because of the form of business organization, or the type of capital used (debt vs. equity, or corporate vs. noncorporate) is achievable at little or no cost. It allows top management to get back to the basic problems of sales and production rather than the artificial complexities imposed by current tax laws.

Many tax theorists argue that it is better to tax consumption expenditures rather than taxing income. This type of taxation results in savings being taxed at a lower rate than consumption. The growth of the economy would be facilitated by a tax law with this characteristic.

There are also tax schemes that result in higher levels of consumption being taxed at higher rates (a progressive consumption tax). The exclusion from taxes of certain consumer goods has also been suggested. We can expect to see an expansion throughout the world in the use of consumption expenditures as the basis of significant taxation. Hopefully, this expansion does not signal an expansion of government spending at the expense of private capital expenditures.

# Chapter 3

# Productivity and the Net Present Value Calculation

It is extremely important that managers properly consider all investment alternatives. If the best investment alternatives are not chosen, the firm is likely to slip to an inferior competitive situation because of inefficiencies caused by using the wrong equipment or wrong production processes. Productivity improvements require that firms evaluate alternatives using the best techniques that are available. One would expect that today 100 percent of professors of finance would recommend for corporations some type of time discounting method, with the net present value method deserving of the top spot.

In this chapter, we will review why firms should evaluate investments using a discounted cash flow (DCF) method especially net present value (NPV) but we will also extend the conventional NPV calculation to include factors that can greatly affect the ability of firms to compete in world markets, and to question some practices that decrease the usefulness of NPV even when it is used as a primary evaluation tool. While this chapter focuses on the NPV method, later we will show that the same opportunities and difficulties apply to the internal rate of return method.

The critics of NPV say that it focuses excessively on short-term considerations. While management may pay excessive attention to the short term, it is not because of the NPV calculation. The NPV calculation takes into consideration the entire life of the investment being considered. While it is true that a dollar to be received at year ten is valued less using NPV than a dollar to be received immediately, no valid economic analysis would do otherwise. Timing of cash outlays and cash inputs has to affect the value of a project. A DCF calculation is an effective way of incorporating the time value of money systematically into the decision process. Future cash flows taking place at time $n$ have to be multiplied by $(1+r)^{-n}$ where $r$ is the appropriate time value factor to find their present value equivalent (it is a trivial change to multiply the cash flows of today by $(1+r)^n$ to find their future value) if we are to evaluate investments in a systematic theoretically correct way. You might be able to evaluate a simple, relatively short-lived investment using a "seaman's eye", but a long-lived asset with changing cash flows through time is much more difficult to evaluate without computing the NPV. It is necessary to do the present value calculations of alternatives in order to make reasonable decisions.

We will define NPV as a method of analyzing investment decisions where future cash flows are brought back to their present value equivalents using a discount rate that appropriately measures the time value of money and reflects the investment's risk. An investment is acceptable if its NPV is equal to or larger than zero. The mechanics of the basic NPV calculation are simple. The steps for evaluating independent investments are:

1. Define the investment's cash flows
2. Define the appropriate discount rate
3. Compute the present values of all cash flows and add all the present values to obtain the NPV
4. Reject the investment if the NPV is less than zero and accept otherwise.

In order to incorporate uncertainty considerations, additional calculations may be made or the above calculations modified, but the core calculations are as described.

Consider an investment of $1,000 that will generate cash flows of $1,210 at time one. The firm can borrow capital at a cost of 0.10.

The net present value of the investment using the firm's 0.10 borrowing rate is:

$$\text{NPV} = \$\text{-}1,000 + \frac{\$1,210}{\$1.10} = \$100$$

and with no risk the investment is acceptable.

With the depreciation expense equal to $1,000 and interest equal to $100, the after interest accounting income at time one will be $1,210 – $1,000 – $100 = $110 which also has a present value of $100 (the equality must occur).

Finally, if we finance the investment earning $1,210 at time one with $1,000 and pay $1,100 interest and principal at time one, we will have $110 at time one in excess of the debt cost. This too has a present value of $100.

The NPV calculation is very powerful in that it does so many things so well. It tells us whether we will have enough funds generated by the investment to repay the debt; and, as illustrated above, it is logically linked to a measure of income.

If an investment costs $1,000 and if we ignore the time value of money, then any future cash flow greater than $1,000 in any time period will be sufficient to justify the investment. But the evaluation process is flawed, because of a failure to consider the cost of money in a theoretical (and practical) manner.

Does this mean that the NPV method of analyzing investments is above criticism? It is possible to use the theoretically correct tool of NPV and use it in such a manner that it gives about as many incorrect decisions as if you had used a known incorrect decision process. There are several types of errors we should be sensitive to, and try to avoid. We will consider the use of an excessively high discount rate.

Continuing the above example, assume the firm wants to earn more than 0.10 because of the high risk level and decides to use a 0.25 discount rate. The NPV is now:

$$\text{NPV} = \$\text{-}1,000 + \frac{\$1,210}{\$1.25} = \$\text{-}32$$

and the investment is not acceptable. It is possible that the investment has so much risk it should be rejected. Or it can be that the investment has so little risk it can be 100 percent financed with 10 percent debt and there is probability one that some positive amount after debt flows will be earned at time one. If the use of the 0.25 required return is arbitrary, the investment will be arbitrarily rejected.

The use of an arbitrary high discount rate by a firm can have disastrous results in evaluating investments with cash flows in the reasonably distant future. The distortions that can be caused by the high discount rate increase the longer the time until the cash is received.

Assume a new innovation in equipment would cost $1,400,000 and would return labor savings of $300,000 per year forever, it can be shown that the present value of a perpetuity of $1 per period is equal to $\frac{1}{\text{interest rate}}$. Thus, with an interest rate of 0.10, the present value of a perpetuity of $1 per year is $10.

If 0.10 is the borrowing rate and if 0.10 is used as the discount rate, we have a net present value of $1,600,000 and the investment is accepted.

PV of benefits:  $300,000\left(\dfrac{1}{0.10}\right) = \$3,000,000$

Immediate outlay:  $\text{NPV} = \dfrac{\$1,400,000}{\$1,600,000}$

But assume the firm has higher aspirations than merely earning its borrowing rate and sets a required return of 0.30, we then have:

$$\$300,000\left(\dfrac{1}{0.30}\right) = \$1,000,000$$

$$\text{NPV} = \dfrac{\$1,400,000}{\$\text{-}400,000}$$

The NPV is negative, and the innovation would be rejected.

Here we have a prime example of NPV being used in a manner that could result in a bad decision. How much risk is there that the $300,000 of savings per year will not occur?

Failure to buy the equipment may result in the firm not being able to compete because its production costs are too high compared to its competitors' costs and may ultimately force it from the market.

There is an extremely high cost in using a decision-making process that employs an excessively high discount rate determined arbitrarily. It is not always a conservative practice. In fact, it may be just the opposite. Using high hurdle rates to evaluate efficiency-type of investments is a very risky investment strategy. It jeopardizes the economic viability of the firm since in the long run rejecting efficiency type of investment may cause the firm to become a high-cost producer.

If firms were to persist in escalating reasonable costs of money upward so that the discount rate did not accurately reflect the cost of the capital being used but rather reflect the artificial goals of management, then it would be valid to say that the use of NPV was not an effective decision process. The rejoinder is that one is not using NPV if the discount rate does not represent the costs of obtaining capital or the returns from investing capital in other uses (the opportunity cost). A firm might be using the formula $(1 + r)^{-n}$ to transform the future cash flows to present values but, if $r$ is not reasonably defined, the numbers obtained are not useful present values and the NPV method is not being used appropriately.

## Other Measures

The entire discussion has been centered on NPV. Another widely used discounted cash flow procedure is the internal rate of return method (IRR). The NPV method leads to a dollar measure of value. Many managers prefer IRR, a percentage measure, because they find they have difficulty interpreting a dollar measure of NPV. They claim it is easier to evaluate an investment if they are told that the investment has an internal IRR of 0.20 than if they are told the net present value is $1,000.

Fortunately, there is no need to disagree on the relative merits of NPV and IRR. In evaluating independent investments with conventional investment-type cash flows, the two measures lead to consistent decisions. There is no essential conflict between NPV and IRR, but there is the possibility of introducing errors into the analysis unless we understand IRR. The basic definition of IRR is that it is the rate of interest that causes the NPV of the investment to be equal to zero. Thus, the IRR is a very special rate of interest, one that leads to a zero net present value for the investment. In the above example, the internal rate of return was 0.21 since:

$$NPV = -1,000 + \frac{1,210}{1.21} = 0$$

If the required return is set arbitrarily at 0.30, the investment would be rejected since the 0.21 IRR is less than the required return. Thus, decision making with either NPV or IRR can be distorted by the use of excessively high discount rates.

## The Next Generation of Investments

Consider a situation where a firm can invest $80,000,000 to modernize or it can shut down the activity. Continuing with the present plant and equipment is not feasible.

A conventional NPV calculation is done and the indicated decision is to shut down (a negative NPV of $5,000,000). What should the firm do?

It is well known that options have either positive or zero value, but not a negative value. Let us consider the NPV analysis for the spending of the $80,000,000 investment. Conventionally, the investment analysis is normally done for a 10-year or a 15-year period. We will assume that the 10-year period is chosen. A residual value is estimated for the $80,000,000 of immediate investment. Frequently, because of expected technological change, the expected salvage value is assumed to be zero.

This type of analysis is deficient since it omits the value of the option to continue the activity at time 10. This option might have a very large value.

Assume that equipment for the process is becoming very automated but that this generation of equipment does not result in a positive net present value. However, expected product design changes and equipment changes are likely in the future. For simplicity, we assume only two outcomes are possible at time 10. Either the product line will be dropped (zero value) or it will be continued with a $100,000,000 value. The zero value has a 0.4 probability and the $100,000,000 value a 0.6 probability. The expected present value (at time 0) of the option to continue the process at time 10 with a 0.10 discount rate is:

$$\text{Expected Present Value} = 0.6(\$100,000,000)\,(1.10)^{-10}$$

$$= \$60,000,000(0.38554) = \$23,133,000$$

The $23,133,000 of expected present value changes the decision from a reject decision because of the $5,000,000 negative net present value to an accept decision with a positive net present value of $18,133,000.

Obviously, the suggested decision process has flaws. Since the next generation of investments is ten years away, and since we have little information now of the activity's value ten years from now, the analyst can place any wild number on the value of the process at time 10.

Rather than directly estimate a value we can compute the expected value needed to break even. In the present example, we need $5,000,000(1.10)^{10} = $12,969,000$ of expected value at time 10 to break even on a present value basis.

We can expect there to be improvements in how we measure the value of the option at time 10 to continue the process. But there will always be the fact that we do not know the future.

One alternative is to cease the operation now because of the negative NPV and then re-enter the game at time 10 if the situation is profitable at that time. Unfortunately, this strategy is very risky because the firm would lose all the opportunities to learn about product design and manufacturing the product if it stopped producing it.

There are large costs of getting out of the game and then attempting to resume the activity.

We conclude that the value of future opportunities have to be brought into the decision process if only on a qualitative basis.

## Conclusions

I stop short of suggesting that DCF calculation will always lead to correct investment decisions. For example, we have not solved the primary problem of applying the net present value method: uncertainty. But with the assumption of certainty we find that the NPV is an extremely powerful tool. If we shifted to an uncertainty assumption, we would find that any sensible procedure would build on some discounted cash flow procedure. One has to take the timing of the cash flows into consideration if sensible investment decisions are to be made.

If we are going to be intelligently critical of practice, then we have to be critical of how any capital budgeting evaluation method is being applied. The use of a DCF method combined with an excessively high discount rate can lead to bad decision making. Ignoring future effects of the decision can also lead to mistakes.

Productivity is harmed when labor and managers are not given competitive plant and equipment with which to work. Good discounted cash flow calculations help lead to good investment decisions and improved productivity.[1]

---

[1] For a more comprehensive discussion of capital budgeting, see Bierman, H. Jr., and S. Smidt (2007). *The Capital Budgeting Decision*, Ninth Edition, Routledge.

# Chapter 4

# A Managerial Incentive Strategy for Increased Productivity

The objective of this chapter is to offer a framework for developing a strategy for rewarding management in a fair and efficient manner. The managerial reward system should supply the maximum incentive for making investment decisions that optimize the well-being of the firm and its shareholders. We want to develop a set of useful numbers on which to base management compensation and to determine whether or not management has done a good or bad job. With widely used conventional measures, a manager doing a good job can have bad performance measures, and a manager doing a bad job can have good performance measures. Equally important, presently used measures can encourage the acceptance of bad investments and the rejection of good investments, thus affecting productivity. In this chapter, we want to define the problems that presently exist in measuring performance. These problems result in productivity being adversely affected, thus require a solution.

We want a system that enables a corporation to identify which divisions should be divested, which should be starved by a restriction of capital expenditures, and which should be force fed to be the next generation of winners. The system is simple. Use the NPV analysis.

Products have life cycles. Imagine a system that identifies when a current product has started to slip in its life cycle and immediately replaces it with another product (a mutually exclusive product) that is just now taking off. The second product's NPV must be larger than that of the first product.

Market share and growth potential are two of the key words. A product's market share and its growth potential determine whether or not it deserves new investment capital. The decisions and strategies flow naturally once the NPV of the cash flow stream of a product (or a division) is computed.

While we stress the use of quantitative measures, we also note the importance of non-quantitative factors and approaches in reaching excellence. One of the quantitative measures widely used is return on investment. It is difficult to find any accounting or finance literature dealing with managerial performance that does not use the return on investment concept. Unfortunately, the ROI measure has severe limitations and I will suggest the use of a better measure.

We have to be careful not to claim too much for any objective quantitative measure of performance. The decision might have been correct but the outcome is not good. Consider the Chairman of the Board of a public utility who starts the construction of a nuclear energy plant expected to cost $3,000,000,000. If the price of a barrel of oil goes from $30 to $90, the Chairman is a hero. But if the price of a barrel of oil dropped to $25 and the cost of the unfinished nuclear energy plant is in excess of $15 billion, the Chairman's performance was not acceptable. With hindsight, we know that mistakes were made. But what will be the evaluation of his performance in twenty years?

There are always unforeseen and uncontrollable events that affect managerial performance measures. If one only uses the quantitative measures without considering the large array of factors affecting those measures, a faulty performance evaluation will be apt to emerge.

## The Problems of Measuring Performance

The paper division earned profits of $100,000,000 and the automotive parts division earned $200,000,000. How much should each of the division managers be paid out of the bonus pool? Which manager did the better job?

One objective of a compensation strategy is to be fair to the managers. A second objective is to motivate the managers to make investment decisions that are best for the corporation. Society benefits from good investment decisions.

It is reasonable to conclude that the methods used to measure performance to reward managers will greatly influence the decisions that are made.

### Problem 1

The firm rewards managers based on the level of the return on investment (ROI). The paper division is currently earning a 0.30 ROI which is the best performance of any of the firm's divisions. The firm has a minimum required return of 0.10.

Assume the division manager of this leading division has an investment opportunity that returns 0.20. If this investment is undertaken, the division's ROI will go from 0.30 to 0.25.

Should the investment be undertaken? Is it likely to be undertaken? If you were the division manager, would you accept it?

We conclude that with the facts as given, there is a large probability of the desirable investment being rejected. This is a mistake given the above information.

### Problem 2

The firm normally requires a 0.10 internal rate of return. A division has an opportunity to undertake an investment that has a return of 0.08, but this investment has much less risk than the firm's normal activities. In fact, the return from this investment is essentially certain. The firm's debt cost is 0.06.

Do we want the division to undertake the investment? How do we get management to seek out and accept these investments?

We recommend the use of lower required returns for investments of lower risk and a careful consideration of the type of investment described.

## Problem 3

The firm is considering two different production lines for making a product. Only one line will be chosen. One has an ROI of 0.20 and the other has an ROI of 0.30; which production line should it acquire? How do we get management to make these decisions correctly?

The economic income calculation to be described in the next chapter tends to solve the problem as does the NPV method of evaluating investments.

## Problem 4

Management wants to maximize growth in earnings per share.

Is this objective reasonable?

Growth is not a sufficient goal. Profitable growth comes closer.

## Problem 5

Management wants to maximize the future stock price of the firm.

Is this a reasonable objective?

We still have to consider the other alternatives available to investors. They might do better with other investments. The firm must consider the investors' opportunity costs.

## Problem 6

A firm is currently earning a 0.15 ROI. Management wants to sell a division that is currently earning 0.10 and increase the firm's ROI to 0.20. Is this restructuring desirable? The firm's cost of debt is 0.06.

The restructuring is not desirable if the risk of the division being sold is minimal.

## Setting Goals

Top management should set profit and ROI goals for the firm and in conjunction with operating management should set goals for divisions. This will include the setting of the targets for dollars of income and ROIs to be earned. Setting goals is one thing; achieving them is another. Consider ways of achieving the basic profit goals. They include:

a.  Cost control, cost reduction, increased productivity and quality: elimination of inefficiency
b.  Improved service and better service than the competitors
c.  Product improvement and innovation
d.  Improved employee morale and thus better productivity
e.  Better and perhaps more selling effort
f.  Obtain assistance (preferential treatment) from the Federal Government or obtain Government business
g.  Better planning (utilization of present resources)
h.  Better investment decisions
i.  In some cases, a modification of the capital structure (debt versus common stock, lease versus conventional debt) might affect income and ROI
j.  Raise or lower prices

We want operating managers to seek out the best choices. The firm needs a sensible incentive system.

## Non-Financial Considerations

We are focusing on the financial measures of performance. This is not to imply that other considerations may not be equally important or even more important.

The famous GM managerial bonus plan was designed so the awards committee had maximum flexibility in making its awards so that it could see beyond the numbers. In the words of the early CEO, Alfred P. Sloan:

> The Bonus Plan established the concept of corporate profit in place of divisional profits, which only incidentally added up to the corporation's net income. Suitably, it provided for bonuses to be paid to

employees "who have contributed to its [General Motors'] success in a special degree by their inventions, ability, industry, loyalty or exceptional service".[1]

What type of factors would you want to consider if you were on the GM awards committee? Consider the following:

What has the division done to maintain product leadership? Are there new products being developed to replace both the maturing products and the products now new, but soon to age?

Is work being done on improving productivity (output and quality)?

Are the different methods of production being effectively investigated?

Are all levels of the employees happy and their morale high? Are their skills being improved?

Is suitable attention being paid to customer loyalty? Are unit sales growing?

Are social responsibilities as defined by the board of directors being met?

Are safety and pollution standards being satisfied not only to the letter of the law, but also to the spirit of the law?

Is the physical plant being suitably maintained?

The above listing of questions is not complete, but it is a reasonable sample of non-financial considerations that should be of interest to top management, and should affect the financial awards of the managers whose performance is being measured.

There are a wide range of problems and issues facing top management as it evaluates its own performance and the performance of divisions. We want to construct a compensation plan and measuring performance strategy for solving the problems described above. We want a procedure that motivates management to make theoretically correct decisions and rewards managers when they make these

---

[1] Alfred P. Sloan, Jr. (1963) *My Years with General Motors*. Doubleday and Company, Inc., New York.

decisions and execute the decisions successfully. The final procedure is likely to be a compromise, but it should be a compromise that comes close to solving as many of the problems that have been described as feasible. We will now consider ROI one of the most widely used and accepted measures of performance. We find it has major deficiencies.

## Return on Investment

ROI is considered by many managers to be the most useful measure of a division's performance, thus there is strong motivation for understanding its limitations. Unfortunately, it has both complexities and flaws.

The basic return on investment calculation consists of dividing an income measure by an investment measure. There are many different methods of computing ROI and many different complexities but we will limit our analysis to limitations that affect investments since investments affect productivity.

## Limitations

Return on investment cannot be used to make investment decisions with any degree of reliability. The basic conventional ROI calculation leaves out the time value of money, thus is fatally flawed for purposes of making investment decisions. Unfortunately, it is used to evaluate investments by many of the Fortune 500 firms.

As a measure of performance, ROI does relate income earned and the amount of investment utilized thus is an appealing measure. This does not completely solve the performance measurement problem since the use of the calculation can distort real decisions that are being made. We will only consider how the use of ROI distorts investment decisions.

## Constant Benefits

Assume an investment costing $497,890 with a life of 30 years will provide constant cash flow benefits of $100,000 per year. This is a

20 percent internal rate of return. Using straight-line depreciation of $16,596, the ROI of year one is:

$$\text{ROI} = \frac{100,000 - 16,596}{497,890} = 0.168$$

The ROI of year 30 is:

$$\text{ROI} = \frac{100,000 - 16,596}{16,596} = 5.03$$

The ROI of the last year is 30 times as large as the ROI of the first year. Interestingly, the problem of understatement of the ROI becomes more dramatic for year one if the life is shorter.

Now assume the life of an asset is five years and the cost $299,060. The cash flows are again $100,000 per year, and the internal rate of return is again 0.20. Continuing to use straight-line depreciation, the ROI of year one is:

$$\text{ROI} = \frac{100,000 - 59,872}{299,060} = 0.134$$

The ROI of year five is:

$$\text{ROI} = \frac{100,000 - 59,872}{59,812} = 0.672$$

When the benefits are increasing through time, the distortion of the operating results in the early years is even larger. Consider the following five-year investment with a 0.20 internal rate of return.

| Time | Cash Flow |
|------|-----------|
| 0 | −50,000 |
| 1 | +12,000 |
| 2 | +14,400 |
| 3 | +17,280 |
| 4 | +20,736 |
| 5 | +24,883 |

Using straight-line depreciation, the incomes and the returns on investment are:

| Period | Beginning Investment | Cash Flow | Straight-line Depreciation | Income | ROI |
|---|---|---|---|---|---|
| 1 | 50,000 | 12,000 | 10,000 | 2,000 | 0.04 |
| 2 | 40,000 | 14,400 | 10,000 | 4,400 | 0.11 |
| 3 | 30,000 | 17,280 | 10,000 | 7,280 | 0.24 |
| 4 | 20,000 | 20,736 | 10,000 | 10,736 | 0.54 |
| 5 | 10,000 | 24,883 | 10,000 | 14,883 | 1.49 |

If the cash flows increased at a faster rate than that shown, the distortion in the ROI would be even larger. The above problem is caused by the use of straight-line depreciation, and it can be solved by the use of more sophisticated depreciation methods. But even a good depreciation method does not solve all the problems involved in its use. The limitations of the conventional ROI measure should be recognized and investment decisions should not be affected by prospective ROI results.

## Problem 1

In Problem 1, we described a situation where a division is currently earning a 0.30 but the division manager is likely to reject a 0.20 investment that will decrease the division's ROI from 0.30 to 0.25. The firm has a required return of 0.10.

The easy solution is to rule that a division must accept the investment because the investment's return is larger than the required return. But we want a procedure where it benefits the division manager to accept an economically desirable investment.

## Problem 6

With Problem 6, we had a situation where the management wants to sell a division in order to increase the firm's ROI. Again, we want a procedure, where the manager is benefited by making the correct decision.

Imagine a system that enabled you to identify which divisions should be divested, which should be starved by a restriction of capital expenditures, and which should be force fed to be the next generation of winners. One way this decision is made is to maximize a measure that we will call a Value Index. This is not a good technique but it is widely used.

The value leverage index is sometimes used to identify those divisions which are doing well (thus deserve capital for expansion) and those divisions which are not doing well and should be divested. Thus an asset redeployment strategy flows from the use of the value leverage index.

What is a value leverage index and how is it used? A plot of different firms shows that the larger the value leverage index the larger the rate of $\frac{\text{Market Value}}{\text{Book Value}}$ of the common stock. If you want a larger ratio of market value to book value, then make decisions to obtain a larger value leverage index.

$$\text{Value Leverage Index} = \frac{\text{Return on Equity}}{\text{Cost of Equity}}$$

One way to increase the Value Index is to divest divisions earning less than the average return on equity capital. Actually, the objective of increasing the Value Index could lead to a strategy of retaining only the one product (or one division) with the largest ratio of return on equity to its cost of equity. Every other product tends to decrease the Value Index. But let us put aside this extreme strategy and investigate the basic evidence that has led to its extensive use.

Observations indicate that when the Value Index is large, the ratio of Market Value to Book Value is large and this appears to be desirable. Therefore, it would appear that one should make decisions that increase the Value Index. This is Asset Redeployment.

But, let us use the basic definition of the Value Index and investigate somewhat more systematically its economic meaning. By definition:

$$\text{Value Index} = \frac{\text{ROE}}{\text{Cost of Equity}}$$

With zero growth and with the firm's market value equal to its economic value, it is not unreasonable to define:

$$\text{Cost of Equity} = \frac{\text{Earnings}}{\text{Market Value}}$$

and

$$\text{ROE} = \frac{\text{Earnings}}{\text{Book Value}}$$

Then substituting these values for $\frac{\text{ROE}}{\text{Cost of Equity}}$, we have for the Value Index:

$$\text{Value Index} = \frac{\frac{\text{Earnings}}{\text{Book Value}}}{\frac{\text{Earnings}}{\text{Market Value}}} = \frac{\text{Market Value}}{\text{Book Value}}$$

Thus, with the reasonable assumption that with the assumed conditions that the $\text{Cost of Equity} = \frac{\text{Earnings}}{\text{Market Value}}$ we find that the Value Index is equal to $\frac{\text{Market Value}}{\text{Book Value}}$. It is not surprising that the larger the Value Index, the larger the ratio of market value to book value. With a reasonable assumption they are equal! They are two ways of saying essentially the same thing.

The Value Index cannot be used effectively for purposes of making asset redeployment decisions. The objective should be to maximize value, not maximize the ratio of market value to book value.

### Asset Redeployment

Assume a firm is considering divesting a division. What are the relevant considerations? The two most important factors to consider are the cash flows that are expected to be earned by operating the division and the amount that can be received if the division is sold.

There may be problems in estimating the future cash flows and in computing a present value equivalent for the flows, but the concept is clear. We want to compare the present value of the different alternatives.

Management might want to inject strategy considerations. While the present value of the cash flows is $100,000,000 and the bid price is only $70,000,000, the firm wants to sell because the division is inconsistent with the corporate plan. Hopefully, the $100,000,000 includes a charge for management time and relevant overhead costs. If it does, then top management has to explain why it is willing to give up $30,000,000 of present value. Of course, another alternative is to continue the search for a bidder who will pay the full value of $100,000,000 or more than $100,000,000.

The analysis for a division that is not a candidate for divestment is analogous. The cash flows should be defined for each strategy that is being considered, and the present value equivalents computed.

If the managers of a product classified as a "dog" that has no growth potential, requests $10,000,000 of capital for plant expansion, they are going to have to present a very strong argument to overcome the initial bias against expanding the productive facilities for a product with no growth potential. They should have the opportunity to present their case.

## Conclusions

It is appropriate for management to make strategic decisions that limit (or expand) the number of different areas of activity that the firm will engage in. Desirable (profitable) investments may be divested if it is felt that their economic viability will be eroded if they are retained since the corporation should put its capital in a different direction.

Asset redeployment can either be made using either the basic cash flow — net present value type of analysis or using a broad strategic type of decision approach where top management decides that corporate strategy dictates more or less capital in a given area.

Rules of thumb that pretend to exactness but have no theoretical foundation should be discarded. A division currently earning a very low ROI may deserve a large amount of new capital and a division that is currently a very high return may not deserve any new capital. The desirability of new expenditures must be determined based on the incremental effects of these new expenditures, not solely on the historical performance of the currently used assets. The NPV calculation should be the basis of any asset redeployment decision.

In the next chapter, we will introduce the economic income measure that solves most of the ROI difficulties. It is an excellent basis on which to reward both management and labor.

To be competitive in a world market, management has to allocate the firm's scarce capital to those activities that have the highest net present value. Without the right capital assets in place to produce goods and services efficiently, a firm will be at a competitive disadvantage that is impossible to overcome. Imagine a group of ten workers with shovels and picks digging a ditch and competing with the driver of a first-class back-hoe. It is no contest.

# Chapter 5

# Economic Income

We want to eliminate the bias against accepting an investment that is expected to earn less than the average return being earned by the firm's other divisions, but more than the firm's required return, and the bias towards divesting desirable profitable divisions that are not expected to grow.

We want a performance measure that will always be increased by a division undertaking and successfully operating an investment that meets the firm's investment acceptance criteria. We will use a NPV criterion to determine if an investment is desirable. We want divisions (and the corporate entity itself) to submit for approval and accept all investments that have positive net present values. We want investments that have desirable economic characteristics to also have favorable performance measurement and incentive pay consequences in order to improve productivity.

A division following an objective of maximization of return on investment can lead to the division rejecting desirable investments. A division currently earning 0.35 ROI will not want to accept an investment that will earn 0.30 if the firm rewards its managers based on the magnitude of the ROI. Even if the firm's required return is only 0.10, there is no incentive to invest in the 0.30 investment if the division's ROI is lowered, with management's compensation then being reduced.

To solve this problem, some firms will combine ROI with growth incentives. This is a step in the right direction but it is extremely difficult to combine ROI and growth measures so that they will always lead to the correct investment decisions for the firm. A management of a division might find it desirable to improve its rewards by increasing growth by accepting an investment even though the investment earns less than the required return.

We recommend the use of economic income as the primary measure of managerial performance. Economic income is in the same position relative to usage as net present value as an investment evaluation tool was in the 1960's. Also, many firms that use economic income for performance measurement use it jointly with ROI. It is not surprising that managers want to know the ROI of an investment center. The relevant question is whether or not the combination of economic income and ROI is being used correctly, with the deficiencies of ROI being effectively controlled by the economic income and growth measures. We define economic income to be the net income after deductions for both depreciation of the asset and an interest expense on the capital used. Other terms used in the past for economic income are residual income and economic value added (EVA).

### Divestments an Opportunity Cost

ROI measures incorrectly used can lead to undesirable divestments. Consider a plant recorded on the books at $200,000,000 that is currently earning $8,000,000 of income (and cash flow) before interest and the plant will earn this amount for perpetuity. The firm requires a 0.10 return so the 0.04 return being earned is not satisfactory. Should the division be divested? Redeployment of assets is frequently recommended in this situation.

To make this decision correctly, we need to know for what price the plant can be sold. Assume the best price offered is $50,000,000.

We now have a present value of $\frac{\$8,000,000}{0.10} = \$80,000,000$ if we retain the plant and $50,000,000 if we sell. The present value advantage of keeping the plant is $30,000,000. While the plant is earning 0.04 based on cost, it is earning $\frac{8,000,000}{50,000,000} = 0.16$ based on the opportunity cost of $50,000,000.

A company should not necessarily dispose of its bad or its good plants and divisions, but rather dispose those assets where the offer price exceeds the present value of expected cash flows.

Consider a division that is currently earning $8,000,000 on book assets of $50,000,000. This is a 0.16 return and well above the 0.10 required return. If a bidder were to offer $120,000,000 the firm should sell (either to this bidder or to a higher bidder) since $120,000,000 is significantly larger than the $80,000,000 present value expected to be earned by operating the plant. The fact that the plant is profitable is not relevant. A marginally larger (than present value) bid should not necessarily be accepted since it is possible that the bidder's value is right and the firm's estimate is wrong.

If a plant (or a division) has negative cash flow and the future cash flow is expected to be negative, then the asset should be sold to the highest bidder. In fact, it can be that the asset should be disposed of even if there is a cash outlay on disposal (we again need to know the present values of the alternatives).

The tendency of a division (or firm) to divest good assets is not easily eliminated by conventional measures of performance. The only sure solution is for top management to review carefully divestment decisions to ensure they are being made for a theoretically correct reason. The NPV of continuing to operate the assets should be compared to the net cash flows of selling.

If conventional book values are used in the measurement of economic income, we can still have economic income measures indicate divestment is desirable when it is not.

Consider the division with $200,000,000 of assets currently earning $8,000,000 before interest. The company has a 0.10 cost of money. The economic income is:

| | |
|---|---|
| Income Before Interest | $8,000,000 |
| Interest Cost (0.10 of $200,000,000) | −$20,000,000 |
| Economic Income | −$12,000,000 |

The economic income is a negative $12,000,000. Should the division be divested? Assume the division can be sold for $50,000,000. The economic income with the asset recorded at $50,000,000 is:

| | |
|---|---|
| Income Before Interest | $8,000,000 |
| Interest Cost (0.10 of $50,000,000) | −$5,000,000 |
| Economic Income | $3,000,000 |

Now the economic income is positive. Since the present value of the cash flows ($80,000,000) is larger than the $50,000,000 that can be obtained by selling, the firm is better off holding than selling. The economic income measure shows that not selling the division is best if the opportunity cost is used as the basis of computing the interest cost of using the assets.

The solution is to abandon the use of cost-based data when that data loses economic significance. If the firm uses cost information when it knows that data does not reflect current values, then the type of decision distortion illustrated by this example will take place, or alternatively management will have to adjust the data on an *ad hoc* basis.

The use of opportunity cost insures that the cost is a relevant cost for the manager whose performance is being measured. Its use eliminates the incentive to manipulate performance measures by divesting overstated assets.

The economic income calculation insures a cost being assigned to capital that is fair, and at the same time, acts as an incentive for management to accept all desirable investments.

Assume the following investment:

| Time | Cash Flow |
|---|---|
| 0 | −3,000 |
| 1 | 1,450 |
| 2 | 1,300 |
| 3 | 1,150 |

If the firm has a 0.10 capital cost, then the economic income measures would be:

|  | Period 1 | Period 2 | Period 3 |
|---|---|---|---|
| Revenue | 1,450 | 1,300 | 1,150 |
| Depreciation | 1,000 | 1,000 | 1,000 |
|  | 450 | 300 | 150 |
| Capital Cost (0.10 of | | | |
| Beginning Investment) | 300 | 200 | 100 |
| Economic Income | 150 | 100 | 50 |

Any investment with an internal rate of return greater than 0.10 will result in an increase to the present value of the economic incomes of the years during the life of the investment.

We can vary the depreciation allocation to each period and change the amount of economic income in each year. But the procedure being used results in a positive present value of economic incomes if the investment has an internal rate of return greater than the firm's capital cost and the expectations are realized.

Following this economic income procedure, if an investment is desirable using the firm's criterion, management benefits if the investment is undertaken and the expectations are realized. If a sensible depreciation method is used in conjunction with economic income, an economic desirable investment (an internal rate-of-return greater than the required return) will lead to a positive economic income in each year.

## Changing Interest Rates

Assume that an investment is undertaken when interest rates are 0.10 but then the rates go up to 0.15. The 0.10 should continue to be used as the capital cost for the basic investment. The investment was undertaken using 0.10 as the required return, and it is reasonable to use the 0.10 as the basic capital cost. Management cannot control the change in interest rates and the change should not cause management to be penalized.

However, we do want working capital decisions to be influenced by the current level of the cost of money. Therefore, the working capital cost should be isolated and the capital costs should reflect the current short-term money costs to the firm.

If there is a change in the management of the investment center, it is reasonable to change the cost basis to its estimated present value, reflecting the new plans of the new management. In addition, the interest rate used should reflect the current cost of long-term capital. The new management will be charged a new "contractual" rate during its tenure.

## Risk Adjustments

The risk level of the asset is likely to be reflected by an increased required discount rate. The increased rate can then be the required capital cost of each period. Thus, the capital cost will reflect both the time value and the risk level of the operating asset whose performance is being measured.

Note that the risk adjustment is being made based on the riskiness of the asset, not the riskiness of the division or of the firm. A very risky division can have a very safe investment. A safe division can have a risky investment.

## The Pay Off

Management should receive as a bonus a percentage of the economic income. The capital contributors are first in line and the managers do not receive a bonus until the basic capital costs are recovered.

Both the capital contributors and the managers share in the good fortune (or good management) that results in excess profits. The economic income measure is not subject to most types of "gaming". By undertaking desirable investments (those with positive net present values), management will increase the firm's economic income over the asset's life as well as their own incomes.

## ROI and Liquidity and Economic Income

It is possible to increase the ROI by increasing sales and increasing income, but in the process harm the firm's liquidity.

Consider a situation where a division is earning 0.20 and the division manager moves to increase the income by giving easier credit. The increased credit results in increased sales and increased income, but the delay in collection causes a cash crunch.

This possibility is controlled in an effective manner by the economic income approach. Management is charged for the increase in working capital, and unless the increase in credit benefits the division by increasing the economic income, there will not be an incentive to increase the amount of credit.

It is true that the economic income effect may be positive, but the firm might still have a liquidity problem. This can be controlled by increasing the capital cost of the working capital so that each dollar increase in working capital pays for itself. If the increased costs assigned to working capital do not lead to a manageable amount of commitments, then other types of controls (including absolute limits on credit) can be implemented to solve short-run liquidity problems.

## One Flaw

Unfortunately, there is a major complexity that is not solved with the economic income procedure.

Management can lead the firm to accept an undesirable risky investment from the viewpoint of risk adverse investors. If the investment has some probability of very desirable outcomes, management, "going for broke", might accept the investment even though the expected value and the risk characteristics of the investment are not favorable for the capital contributors. The economic income calculations do not cope with this type of situation very well.

Top management and the board of directors both have the responsibility of minimizing this type of speculation. Also, we can expect most managers to consider their own interest and the interests of the investors to coincide more than is implied by the above description.

Another variation of this problem of evaluating risky investments is where a risk avoiding management rejects an investment that the investors would prefer to have accepted, if they had all the facts. This problem of coping with risk does exist for the suggested economic income procedure, but it also exists for all other commonly used procedures.

## Quality Points

Most firms have more complex objectives than some form of profit maximization. They also want to achieve a wide range of firm and social objectives. This can include social objectives such as community involvement by management or target employment mix goals or firm objectives such as training employees and developing new products.

Whatever these other goals, top management should place dollar measures on them so that operating management is rewarded for meeting them or is penalized for not meeting them.

Management then decides on how much should be spent to meet the corporate goals of a non-profit or long-run profit nature.

There are many experts who would argue that non-economic goals are inappropriate for a publicly held corporation. This is not the appropriate place for arguing the merits of such goals. We can conclude that if such goals are appropriate, the suggested economic income procedure can readily incorporate the goals into the performance measurement and incentive compensation procedure.

## Economic Income and Net Present Value

One attractive feature of the economic income measure is that the present value of the economic incomes is equal to the net present value of the investment with zero residual values of the asset.

Consider the investment with the following cash flows:

| Time | Cash Flow |
|------|-----------|
| 0 | −3,000 |
| 1 | 1,450 |
| 2 | 1,300 |
| 3 | 1,150 |

The investment's net present value using a discount rate of 0.10 is $256.57. We previously computed the economic incomes. Their present value using 0.10 is also $256.57.

| Period | Economic Income | Present Value Factors | Present Values |
|--------|-----------------|-----------------------|----------------|
| 1 | 150 | $1.10^{-1}$ | 136.36 |
| 2 | 100 | $1.10^{-2}$ | 82.64 |
| 3 | 50 | $1.10^{-3}$ | 37.57 |
|   |   | Net Present Value | $256.57 |

This result is nice since it reconciles the discounted cash flow method of making investment decisions and the method of measuring income each period.

While a specific theoretically sound method of depreciation may be preferred, the equality of the discounted cash flow net present value and the present value of economic incomes will hold for any method of depreciation. The crucial component of the calculation is to include the capital cost on the asset being used.

## Comparisons of Divisions

We have suggested the use of economic income, but does the use of economic income facilitate the comparison of two or more divisions?

Assume one division (Division A) has $900,000 of economic income and a second division (Division B) has $1,000,000 of economic income. Which division is better managed (assume no accounting complexities exist)?

Suppose if Division A has $10,000,000 of assets and Division B has $400,000,000 of assets. Are these asset value measures relevant in determining whether or not A has better performance than B, given the above economic income measures?

The economic income measure includes the size of the assets utilized since that size determines the amount of interest that will be charged. It is not necessary to bring in the size of assets a second time. In fact, if this is done, the measure moves closer to being an ROI measure, with all the faults of ROI.

Let us consider the amount of income before interest that has to be earned by the two divisions described above. Assume the firm has a 0.10 cost of money.

|  | Division A<br>Assets = $10,000,000 | Division B<br>Assets = $400,000,000 |
|---|---|---|
| Income Before Interest | $1,900,000 | $41,000,000 |
| Interest Cost | $1,000,000 | $40,000,000 |
| Economic Income | $900,000 | $1,000,000 |

Note that the income before interest measures are greatly affected by the magnitude of the assets used. Division B needs $40,000,000 of income before interest but A only needs $1,000,000 to break even. The interest cost measure adequately reflects the amount of assets used.

We can say that the management of Division B did a better job since they received the required return of $40,000,000 on the capital utilized and in addition they earned $1,000,000 of excess income.

The management of A recovered the required return of $1,000,000 on the capital utilized and in addition they earned $900,000 of excess income.

If we evaluate the performance of management by relating the economic income to the amount of investment, then we have circled back to ROI with the faults of ROI still remaining.

ROI is a very attractive measure since it has universal meaning. A one-period return of 0.10 on $100 has the same economic meaning as a one-period return of 0.10 on $1,000,000. With a $100 investment, a 0.10 return implies period one income of $10 and with a $1,000,000 investment, a return of 0.10 implies income of $100,000. Percentage returns are part of everyday life, and everyone understands them to some extent.

The ROI measure, being a percentage, can be compared easily to the firm's cost of capital and conclusions can be reached about the adequacy of the return. But the ROI measure has its deficiencies. Improving a division's ROI by divesting a subunit that is earning less than the average ROI is feasible but may not be desirable. A similar decision is to reject a new investment that earns less than the division is currently earning but is otherwise acceptable to the firm. While the use of economic income solves these problems, ROI is widely used and management has to be aware of its deficiencies.

## Continuity of Firm's Existence

It is possible that an investment opportunity has a positive NPV using expected cash flows but that a risk analysis shows that project jeopardizes the firm's existence. If the probabilities of bad outcomes and the size of the bad outcomes is too large, management should not base the final decision on the expected NPV but should apply a thoughtful decision analysis that allows project rejection if the risk analysis shows too high a level of bad outcomes.

## Conclusions

We are searching for a performance measure which goes up when efficiency goes up and where management has an incentive to accept economically desirable investments. The suggested economic income procedure does give management an incentive to invest in all economically desirable investments.

There is a problem involving investments with undesirable risk characteristics. A risk-taking management might undertake investments that are not acceptable to investors. A risk-avoiding management might reject investments that the investors would want the firm to accept. These problems are not solved by the suggested procedure, but they are not harmed by it. These types of problems involving risk require separate solutions.

# Chapter 6

# Flexible Wages: A Wage Plan for Increased Productivity

We will initially consider the normal wage contract made by labor. Labor is conventionally paid a fixed amount per hour and the firm (and worker) then determines the number of hours that are worked.

Let us assume that the hourly wage rate is $20 per hour and that a product requires five hours of labor (a total labor cost per unit of $100). If the product sells for less than $100 (say, $80), management will not produce and the five hours of labor will be lost or will be used elsewhere. Assume the next best use of the specific labor is $5 per hour (the next best use could be zero). The economic value of the labor for five hours becomes $25 rather than $80 of labor costs which would have been the result if the product had been produced.

Instead of charging $20 per hour, assume that labor charges its opportunity cost of $5 per hour and the product cost is now $25 per unit. If a unit brings in $80 of revenue, and if the cost is $25, the units will be produced and sold.

If labor receives all or part of the $55 incremental profit, labor is better off working for $5 per hour plus a profit sharing bonus than not working for $20 per hour. We want to evolve a system of paying labor that reduces the fixed hourly cost to labor's opportunity cost, and then rewards labor with a share of the firm's excess (or economic) profits.

We do not mean to imply that this plan is for all firms, but it should be useful for a wide range of firms.

## The Solution

The solution to many productivity problems is pay labor a basic labor rate equal to some minimum rate and supplement the minimum amount with a percentage of the firm's excess income. We will also pay management a fixed minimum amount and have the remainder of the managerial pay a function of profitability.

Assume that using the minimum wage rate the firm earned basic income after wages of $10,000,000 and the stock equity is $50,000,000. The basic stock equity return to be targeted is 0.12 or $6,000,000.

The excess return earned is $4,000,000 to be split between labor, stock equity, and management.

## Issues to be Resolved

The issues to be resolved are:

a. The basic minimum hourly wage rate
b. The basic return on the stock equity
c. The split of the excess income between labor, stock equity, and management
d. Which excess (residual) income is to be split.

## Basic Minimum Hourly Wage

The easiest and most objective fixed wage rate measure to use is the minimum hourly wage specified by federal law. But the effective minimum rate could be higher or lower than this rate.

Let us assume that the minimum wage is defined to be $5. Congress would be implying that it would rather see workers unemployed than work for any amount less than $5. It can be logically argued that a minimum wage amount established by law is not a desirable thing. But given the existence of the minimum amount, it can be used as a type of opportunity cost (especially if it is illegal to pay less than the minimum in any event).

Would a worker currently earning $20 per hour be willing to give up that theoretical wage to work for $5 per hour? We would expect the initial reaction to be a flood of four-letter words, but let us do some arithmetic. Assume the following facts:

Working for $20 per hour: $20 × 500 hours = $10,000 per year
Working for $5 per hour: $5 × 1,500 hours = $ 7,500
plus: profit bonus                          = _____?
                                              $ 7,500 + ? per year

Is $5 per hour better for the worker than $20? It depends on the hours worked and the size of the profit bonus.

It cannot be guaranteed that workers will be better off in annual take-home pay with the lower hourly rate, but it is very likely.

In addition to the problem of the magnitude of the total annual wage, there is also the cash flow problem. This can be solved by having the bonus for a quarter determined by the earnings of the quarter two periods ago and then having the earnings adjusted for the final annual earnings.

The sequence could be as follows:

| | Quarter | | | | | |
|---|---|---|---|---|---|---|
| | 1 | 2 | 3 | 4 | 5 | 6 |
| Reported Earnings | Q1 | Q2 | Q3 | Q4 | Q5 | Q6 |
| Wages Determined by | | | Q1 | Q2 | Q3 | Q4 |

When the annual earnings for Q1 to Q4 are determined in Quarter 5, there would be an adjustment that would be spread over the next four quarters. Most importantly, there are a large number of ways for spreading the bonus amount over all pay periods so that the take-home pay is more than $5. The method of calculation insures the wage rate will not be less than $5 (losses are not shared). It can be greater than $20 per hour. With a firm that has excess profits in each quarter, the worker always takes home more than $5 per hour.

### Basic Return on the Stock Equity

The amount to be paid to the stock equity before arriving at the bonus amount is not the result of an exact clearly defined calculation. It picks up all the complexities of the fair return to be allowed a regulated public utility's stock equity.

Also, the entire economic income is not to fall to labor but rather the economic income is to be split between labor, management, and stock equity.

One solution is to use relatively large amounts of preferred stock in the capital structure. The preferred stock has a contractually defined dividend, thus there is an objective contractually defined amount that has to be deducted before obtaining the economic income.

It is the common stock that offers the difficulty. How much should the common stock get before labor gets a kicker above the minimum wage? One sensible solution is to pay the stockholders a minimum amount where the minimum is defined as being equal to the return being earned on some type of fixed income security, say a single A bond. This is conceptually equivalent to labor's minimum hourly wage.

### The Split

We have now computed an economic income for the corporation. That economic income is to be split between labor, management, and stockholders. So far, each has received less than they think they deserve. Labor and management have received minimum amounts and the common stock has received the return usually attributed to investors in much less risky debt. If the split of the economic income is not fair to common stock investors, the firm will have difficulty raising common stock capital. The same type of reasoning applies to labor and to management. All of the three sectors require the expectation of fair treatment. We do not have to define more exactly the specific terms of the split (nor are we capable of defining it). But whatever the agreed split, all three components have the incentive to maximize the economic income. All actions should be consistent with that maximization. Bad investment decisions by management will harm residual income as will strikes by labor. There will be strong incentives to produce and sell products as long as the incremental revenues exceed the incremental costs.

## Which Profit?

With a single product firm there is no problem defining the profit that is of interest. It is the economic income of the firm.

If the firm has several divisions and many plants, then we have to decide on the profit measurement that is to be split. If each plant were a well-defined profit center with well-defined assets used by the plant, and if no costs were allocated to the plant, then the economic profit of the plant could be used.

If we shift to a division of the firm, the same type of conclusion holds. We can use the profits of the division as the basis of the split if there are no cost allocations or joint utilization of facilities.

But the more likely situation is that the financial affairs of the plants, divisions, and firm are all interwoven. The profit measures of the plant, division, and firm are somewhat subjective.

The proposed solution is to base the bonus for labor and management on the economic income of all the profit units. That is, the profit of the plant, the profit of the division and the profit of the firm would all affect the wage and managerial bonuses.

For example, assume the following facts apply:

| | Economic Income of Plants | Minimum Wage Amounts | | Economic Income of Divisions |
|------|------|------|------|------|
| A | 40,000 | 10,000 | I | 100,000 |
| B | 60,000 | 40,000 | | |
| C | 80,000 | 90,000 | II | 200,000 |
| D | 120,000 | 40,000 | | |
| E | 0 | 70,000 | | |
| Firm | 300,000 | 250,000 | | 300,000 |

If the bonuses were computed using plant residual profits, the workers of plant E would receive no bonus. But all the workers of both divisions and of the firm would receive a bonus if the bonuses were based on division or firm economic incomes.

Assume the firm's workers are to receive 50 percent or $150,000 as a bonus. The total wage bonus is based on the firm's economic income. It is further decided that 0.20 or $30,000 will be based on firm's profits, 0.50 or $75,000 on division profits, and 0.30 or $45,000 on plant profits.

Using the minimum wage amounts, we have for the allocation of the $30,000:

|   | Relative Amount of Wages | Bonus Amount | Plant Bonus |
|---|---|---|---|
| A | 0.04 | 30,000 | 1,200 |
| B | 0.16 | 30,000 | 4,800 |
| C | 0.36 | 30,000 | 10,800 |
| D | 0.16 | 30,000 | 4,800 |
| E | 0.28 | 30,000 | 8,400 |
|   | 1.00 |  | 30,000 |

The $75,000 will be split $\frac{1}{3} \times \$75,000 = \$25,000$ to division I and $\frac{2}{3} \times \$75,000 = \$50,000$ to division II. If these amounts are then allocated using amounts of minimum wages, we then have:

|   | Relative Amount of Wages | Bonus Amount | Bonus |
|---|---|---|---|
| A | 0.20 | 25,000 | 5,000 |
| B | 0.80 | 25,000 | 20,000 |
| C | 0.45 | 50,000 | 22,500 |
| D | 0.20 | 50,000 | 10,000 |
| E | 0.35 | 50,000 | 17,500 |
|   |  |  | 75,000 |

The $45,000 would be split based on plant profits:

|   | Profits | Proportion | Amount | Bonds |
|---|---------|-----------|--------|-------|
| A | 40,000 | 0.13 | 45,000 | 5,850 |
| B | 60,000 | 0.20 | 45,000 | 9,000 |
| C | 80,000 | 0.27 | 45,000 | 12,150 |
| D | 120,000 | 0.40 | 45,000 | 18,000 |
| E | 0 | | 45,000 | 0 |
|   | 300,000 | | | 45,000 |

Workers and management should all realize that they have loyalty to plants, divisions, and firms and the profitability of each affects their incomes.

## The Share Economy

Martin Weitzman has introduced *The Share Economy*.[1] While Weitzman indicates that he is not committed to anyone specific calculation for wages, he does want wages to be a function of activity. For example, he illustrates his position with an example where employees receive as compensation a two-thirds share of a firm's average revenue per worker.[2]

We suggest that additions to minimum wages be a function of profit after a minimum return to capital. First labor receives a basic wage and then equity capital receives a basic return on its investment, and then a sharing takes place. The wage rate and the return to equity capital are flexible and a function of the firm's profitability.

Weitzman's use of revenue (a gross measure) has the advantage of being better defined than the accounting measure of profits that we use. Accounting measures of profit have some elements of arbitrariness that can cause distrust.

However, we want management to have an incentive to make the decisions that tend to increase profits. Paying workers a fraction of

---

[1] Martin L. Weitzman (1984). *The Share Economy.* Cambridge, MA: Harvard University Press.
[2] Ibid., pp. 4–5.

incremental profits will cause management to act in a manner that will increase profits.

If workers are paid as a fraction of revenues, it is possible for management to reject business that would be profitable with a different arrangement.

**Example**

Assume the following situation and possible changes:

|  | Present Situation | Results After Proposed Change |
|---|---|---|
| Revenue | $1,000,000 | $3,000,000 |
| Expenses | $300,000 | $1,000,000 |
| Profit Before Wages | $700,000 | $2,000,000 |
| Number of Workers | 10 | 15 |
| Revenues per Worker | $100,000 | $200,000 |
| Wage Bill per Worker | $66,667 | $133,333 |
| Total Wage Bill | 666,667 | 2,000,000 |
| Net Income | 33,333 | 0 |

The Weitzman proposal leads management to reject the proposed change. Using our proposal and a zero basic wage and return to equity and an income split with the present situation that leads to $666,667 total wages, we have:

|  | Present Situation | Proposed Change |
|---|---|---|
| Revenue | $1,000,000 | $3,000,000 |
| Expenses | $300,000 | $1,000,000 |
| Profit | $700,000 | $2,000,000 |
| To Workers (0.9524): | $666,667 (0.9524): | $1,905,000 |
| To Capital (0.0476): | 33,333 (0.0476): | 95,000 |
| Wage per Worker | $66,667 | $127,000 |

While the present situation is unchanged, both the workers and the firm are better off with the proposed change.

The exact nature of the split can be somewhat different than that discussed above but still retain the advantage of using the profit measure as the basis for the split. There are many different ways of achieving the objective of making labor a true variable cost, variable with respect to the rate as well as the hours worked.

## When Does It Apply?

When is the flexi wage plan most useful? Consider a steel plant in Utah where the hourly wage cost is $25 per hour. Labor has no alternative in that area. With a labor cost of $25 per hour, the plant cannot break even and the plant will be closed. Flexi wage would give management and labor a chance to turn the situation around.

In the above Utah steel plant situation, the fixed hourly wage cost was high and labor is a significant part of total costs. These two characteristics make the flexi wage arrangement desirable.

At the other extreme would be a situation where labor is a very small percentage of the total expenses and capital is a very important part of the process. In addition, the equity investment has a large amount of risk. In this situation, it might be more desirable to define the labor cost exactly in terms of a fixed hourly rate. There may be only a small likelihood of a large profit and a large amount of risk for the equity participants. The equity capital would not be happy about sharing the large profits, but bearing all the risks. Thus, the plan might not offer obvious advantages in all situations but it is well worthwhile considering.

## The A&P Case[3]

In 1869, a firm engaged in the importing of tea from China named itself The Great Atlantic and Pacific Tea Company, Inc. in recognition

---

[3] This section is based on the case "A&P's James Wood Tried to Turn Grandma Around" written by G.P. Watson and L.D. Alexander of Virginia Polytechnic Institute and State University.

of the fact that tea landing on the west coast of the United States could at last be shipped east by railroad. The firm rapidly expanded its product line and by 1925 A&P sales for its 14,000 stores totaled $440,000,000. In the 1960's, it reached its maximum profitability and then competition rapidly eroded its profitability. In 1979, when a German food merchandiser took control of 50.7 percent of the company's stock, the company had suffered a series of loss years.

In 1979, James Wood was hired to make A&P profitable again. Approximately one-half of his salary was contingent on the firm's performance. He was also given an option to buy 10 percent of the outstanding stock at $4 per share.

One of the major problems facing Wood was the fact that A&P's labor costs were high and union contracts controlled many decisions. For example, if a store was closed, the higher paid older workers of that store would bump the lower paid younger workers of a second store.

Wood solved that problem by closing entire divisions, thus escaping the seniority rules. The unions realized that the company was fighting for its life and made concessions. For example, in 1982, the local union in Philadelphia conceded 25 percent of their wages and benefits but would recover as a wage supplement 1 percent of their store's sales as long as labor costs were 10 percent of sales or less. Before the cost concession, labor costs were 15 percent of sales.

In 1981, the A&P lost $102 million (in 1980, the loss was $43 million) but in 1982, the net income was $31 million; in 1983, it was $48 million. The turnaround in profits did not result because of the above labor arrangement, but it is interesting that the changed pay arrangement and the increased profits both occurred.

### The Investment Banking Community

The investment banking community is the best example of a flexible wage system for its professional staff. Investment bankers are paid reasonable but not excessively high hourly wages. They have high salaries but they work long hours and on a purely hourly basis, they do not do all that well. Where they win is with the annual bonus paid in January or February. If their operating unit and the firm both do well, they will share in the well being.

This wage system makes it easier for the firm to shrink its wage bill in a bad year without massive layoffs. The investment bankers are aware that a bad year means little or no bonus. Good years make up for the bad years.

The firm can experiment with new ideas and new people since the fixed cost of hiring is relatively low. Only if the people or the idea is successful, does the wage bill become large.

## Conclusions

Under the proposed plan, labor will earn an amount (an hourly wage) equal to or more than their minimum but probably less than the current hourly rate (but maybe more). The total amount earned in a year by labor is likely to be larger under the plan than without the plan.

Management's pay will be tightly tied to performance. Managers whose firm division or plant performs badly from a profit perspective will not be well paid.

Stockholders will have a reasonably high probability of earning the equivalent of a bond return (say a single A bond), and a somewhat lower probability of significantly exceeding that bond rate.

The total output of the firm will be larger with the proposed pay system than without it, since the hourly wage that is defined for the production is much lower than the current rate and the firm will be able to charge lower prices for its products. If productivity is measured in total over a period of time, it will be larger with the proposed pay system than without it.

# Chapter 7

# Industrial Democracy

Long ago someone decided that it was desirable that management should have significant stock ownership in the corporation for which it worked. The amount of ownership and the level of management that was eligible to participate varied widely from corporation to corporation. But it was widely accepted that hourly employees were paid wages for their contributions to the firm's profits and there was no need for these employees to participate in the ownership. In this chapter, I will critically review this conclusion and consider some alternative opinions that have been offered through the years. You may well be surprised by a bit of the history.

The title of this chapter is taken from an address given by Louis Brandeis before the National Congress of Charities and Correction in Boston in June 8, 1911.

Louis Brandeis (1856–1941) graduated from Harvard Law School and was appointed to the U.S. Supreme Court in 1916 by President Woodrow Wilson (he was the first Jew to be appointed to that court). He devoted his entire life and career to public causes (social issues) such as free speech and the right to privacy. His positions are often upsetting (inconsistent with the status quo), but always thought provoking.

The first paragraph of his address follows[1]:

Politically, the American workingman is free — so far as the law can make him so. But is he really free? Can any man be really free

---

[1] Alfred Lief and Charles A. Beard (1930). *The Social and Economic Views of Mr. Justice Brandeis*, New York: The Vanguard Press.

who is constantly in danger of becoming dependent for mere subsistence upon somebody and something else than his own exertion and conduct? Financial dependence is consistent with freedom only where claim to support rests upon right, and not upon favor.

In a later address before the United States Commission on Industrial Relations (April 16, 1914 and January 23, 1915), he expanded on his 1911 address[2]:

It seems to me that the intensive study of businesses and of the elimination of wage in business must result in regularizing business. Every man who has undertaken to study the problem of his business in the most effective way has come to recognize that what we must do is to keep the business running all the time, keep it full. If it is a retail business, he makes it his effort to make other days in the week than Saturday a great day; he tries to take periods of the year when people do not naturally buy and make them buy, in the off seasons, in order to keep his plant going during the period in which ordinarily and in other places of business it loses money. Now, that effort must proceed in every business, to try by means of invention, and invention involving large investment, to make the business run throughout the year; that is, to regularize the work, avoid the congestion of the extra-busy season, and avoid the dearth in what has been a slack season. ...

This concern is consistent with the flexi-wage plan offered in Chapter 6. Brandeis disavows profit sharing as a solution.[3] I do not understand the inclusion of the word "merely".

Profit sharing, however liberal, cannot meet the situation. That would merely mean dividing the profits of business.

---

[2] Ibid., pp. 381–382.
[3] Ibid., pp. 383.

Brandeis is thinking beyond monthly pay.[4]

There must be a division not only of profits, but a division also of responsibilities. The employees must have the opportunity of participating in the decisions as to what shall be their condition and how the business shall be run. They must learn also in sharing that responsibility that they must bear, too, the suffering arising from grave mistakes, just as the employer must. But the right to assist in making the decisions, the right of making their own mistakes, if mistakes there must be, is a privilege which should not be denied to labor. We must insist upon labor sharing the responsibility for the result of the business.

Brandeis is not in favor of workers gaining power (achieving the stated objectives) via the ownership of stock.[5]

From the standpoint of the community, the welfare of the community, and the welfare of the workers in the company, what is called a democratization in the ownership through the distribution of stock is positively harmful. Such a wide distribution of the stock dissipates altogether the responsibility of stockholders, particularly of those with five shares, ten shares, fifteen shares, or fifty shares. They must recognize that they have no influence in a corporation of hundreds of millions of dollars capital. Consequently, they consider it immaterial whatever they do, or omit to do. The net result is that the men who are in control is almost impossible to dislodge, unless there be such a scandal in the corporation as to make it clearly necessary for the people on the outside to combine for self-protection. Probably even that necessity would not be sufficient to ensure a new management. That comes rarely, except when those in control withdraw because they have been found guilty of reprehensible practices resulting in financial failure. ...

---

[4] Ibid., pp. 383.
[5] Ibid., pp. 384.

The wide distribution of stock, instead of being a blessing, constitutes, to my mind, one of the gravest dangers to the community. It is absentee landlordism of the worst kind.

Thus, the most liberal of scholars is against the workers attempting to gain power by stock ownership. He goes on to state[6]:

Industrial democracy will not come by gift. It has got to be won by those who desire it. And if the situation is such that a voluntary organization like a labor union is powerless to bring about the democratization of a business, I think we have in this fact some proof that the employing organization is larger than is consistent with the public interest. I mean by larger, is more powerful, has a financial influence too great to be useful to the State; and the State must in some way come to the aid of the workingmen if democratization is to be secured.

Men must have industrial liberty as well as good wages.

We cannot claim that Brandeis would have agreed with the thrust of this chapter, but he desires the same objectives.

## Andrew Carnegie

Andrew Carnegie (1835–1911) was an American (of Scottish birth) leader of industry. He created the Carnegie Steel Company which was later to be changed into U.S. Steel Corporation. Carnegie devoted the last years of his life to philanthropy. He is famous for financing local libraries throughout the United States but he also founded the Carnegie Corporation of New York, Carnegie Endowment for International Peace, Carnegie Mellon University, etc.

However, his record has a significant blot that affected his thinking about labor. In 1892, the famous Homestead Strike took place at Carnegie Steel's plant in Homestead Pennsylvania. The strike lasted

---

[6] Ibid., pp. 385.

143 days and there were ten deaths and hundreds were injured. The extracts that follow were published in 1908. The thrust of his writings is captured by "the next step toward improved labor conditions is through the stage of shareholding in the industrial world..."

Andrew Carnegie accomplished much good in his lifetime and laid the foundation for doing good for as long as history is recorded. The book to be cited was published in 1908, thus preceded Brandeis' talks.

The following quotation gives us Carnegie's philosophy[7]:

> Labor, Capital, and Ability are a three-legged stool. There is no first, second, or last. There is no precedence! They are equal members of the great triple alliance which moves the industrial world. ...

Carnegie's grand plan is to have Labor as shareholders.[8]

> Labor is to rise still higher. The joint-stock form opens the door to the participation of Labor as shareholders in every branch of business. In this, the writer believes, lies the final and enduring solution of the Labor question. The Carnegie Steel Company made a beginning by making from time to time forty-odd young partners, only one was related to the original partners, but all were selected upon their proved merits after long service. None contributed a penny. Their notes were accepted, payable only out of the profits of the business.

Carnegie expected that stock ownership would change attitudes[9]:

> Every employee a shareholder would prevent most of the disputes between Capital and Labor, and this chiefly because of the feeling of mutuality which would be created, now, alas! generally lacking. To effect this, every corporation could well afford to sell shares to its saving workmen, giving preference in repayment at cost as a first

---

[7] Andrew Carnegie (1908). *The Problems of Today: Wealth-Labor-Socialism.* Doubleday, Page and Company, New York.

[8] Ibid., pp. 54.

[9] Ibid., pp. 56.

charge in case of disaster, just as present laws provide first for the mechanic's lien and for homestead exemption. This is due to the workingman, who necessarily buys the shares without knowledge, and he is asked to buy them, not solely for his own advantage, but for the benefit of the company as well — the advantage of both.

A later variation of the plan guaranteed the workers against loss.[10] Not everyone would agree with this provision. But Carnegie believed strongly in the ownership of shares by labor.[11]

The writer, however, believes one point to be clear, viz. that the next step toward improved labor conditions is through the stage of share-holding in the industrial world, the workman becoming joint owner in the profits of his labor. ... What the workingman has to consider, and consider well, is whether this is not the most advantageous path for him to continue to tread. So far as it has been tried it has proved a decided success, and it can easily be continued since it is proving mutually beneficial to Capital and Labor. One of the greatest advantages, the writer thinks, will be found in drawing men and managers into closer intercourse, so that they become friends and learn each other's virtues, for that both have virtues none knows better than the writer, who has seen both sides of the shield as employee and employer.

So far, we have Brandeis opposed to worker ownership of the stock of the employer and Carnegie who tried it and found it worked. Now, we go to the very liberal William O. Douglas.

## William O. Douglas

William O. Douglas (1892–1980) was a civil libertarian who also sat on the U.S. Supreme Court. It is said that he was a more committed

---

[10] Ibid., pp. 59–61.
[11] Ibid., pp. 65–66.

civil libertarian than Louis Brandeis but the current author suspects that Brandeis is more than competitive on that dimension. Douglas actually replaced Brandeis on the Supreme Court.

Douglas was the third Chairman of the Securities and Exchange Commission (1937–1939).

There were two attempts to remove Douglas from the Supreme Court. Both attempts were not successful. They were both based on differences with Douglas' intellectual positions and political considerations, not because of unethical acts by him. Douglas attracted controversy.

The first paragraph of "Corporation Management" (and the subsequent paragraphs) was written before 1940 but it applies with no changes to the present time and subsequent years. Consider "Responsible management has always recognized its position as the servant of the stockholders". Check out the conversions of public corporations (e.g., Quintiles, B-Way, etc.) into private equity in recent years and see if in these cases management was a servant of the stockholders.

In an address before the International Management Congress in Washington, D.C., September 27, 1938, Douglas stated:[12]

> Responsible management has always recognized its position as the servant of the stockholders. Yet the blight of capitalism has been a specious brand of morality for corporations, a morality which drew a distinction between the allegiance which the management demanded of its staff and the allegiance which management owed to its stockholders. There can be no such distinction. Once capitalism forsakes the standards of trusteeship, it bids fair to destroy itself. It is the job of such agencies as the Securities and Exchange Commission to eradicate that specious brand of morality and to restore old-fashioned standards which place business above suspicion or reproach for questionable financial practices.

---

[12] James Allen, *Democracy and Finance, The Addresses and Statements of William O. Douglas*, pp. 57.

He then focuses on the responsibility of management to stock-holders.

> Service to stockholders cannot be a passive thing. It is not some-thing to be rendered with the lips. It calls for constant diligence and tireless devotion to the standards of fiduciary responsibility upon which our capitalistic system is based. It is not enough to make an honest and revealing annual report. Management must, in every act, inspire the confidence of investors whose funds are its lifeblood. For, if the American public has a large stake in the country's corporate business, so American corporations have their stake in the public confidence. It is in that respect that this part of the President's pro-gram has its greatest significance to those who believe in capitalism and democracy.

Douglas wants to improve the relationship of management and the public but he does not consider the issue of labor and stock own-ership. This is disappointing since he was in a position to influence both investors (stockholders) and labor (he had its respect).

To return to the issue of worker stock ownership, we turn to one of the two or three leading American industrialists of the twentieth century as well as one of the leading statesmen, Owen D. Young.

## Owen D. Young

Owen D. Young (1879–1962) was a great American industrialist becoming GE's president in 1922 and was president until 1939. In 1929, he was named "Time Magazine's Man of the Year".

Young extensively advised five U.S. presidents from 1920 to 1939. In 1932, he was a leading candidate for the Democratic Presidential nomination (awarded to Franklin Roosevelt). From 1924 to 1929, he served on several international committees with his agenda being to reduce the amount of German reparations. He was only partially successful, but he tried.

The following extracts from his biography Owen D. Young and American Enterprise by Josephine Young Case and E.N. Case give us a window into the mind of Owen D. Young regarding the status of labor and large corporations. In May 1926, Young addressed the National Electric Light Association and stated[13]:

> You are not afraid of new inventions and new engineering in your physical plants... May I suggest that invention, improved engineering and courage to take the road are needed now more in the social than in the physical sciences. *I recommend that we take the overhead of research and experiment in the social field now when the social balance sheet is stable and not postpone them to the day when it may be too late.*

On June 4, 1927, Young gave the principal address at the Harvard Graduate School of Business Administration's dedication of its new Baker Building.[14]

> Perhaps some day we may be able to organize the human beings engaged in a particular undertaking so that they truly will be the employer buying capital as a commodity in the market at the lowest price. It will be necessary for them to provide an adequate guaranty fund in order to buy their capital at all. If that is realized, the human beings will then be entitled to all the profits over the cost of capital.
>
> I hope the day may come when these great business organizations will truly belong to the men who are giving their lives and their efforts to them, I care not in what capacity. Then they will use capital truly as a tool and they will all be interested in working it to the highest economic advantage. Then an idle machine will mean to every man in the plant who sees it as an unproductive charge against himself. Then every piece of material not in motion will mean to the man who sees it as an unproductive charge against himself. Then we shall have zest in labor, provided the leadership is competent and the division fair. Then we shall dispose, once and for all, of the charge

---

[13] Josephine Young Case and Everett Needham Case, *Owen D. Young and American Enterprise, A Biography*, David R. Godina, Boston, 1982, pp. 371.

[14] Ibid., pp. 374.

that in industry organizations are autocratic and not democratic. Then we shall have all the opportunities for a cultural wage which the business can provide. Then, in a word, men will be as free in cooperative undertakings and subject only to the same limitations and chances as men in individual businesses. Then we shall have no hired men.

## The Consequences of Young's Address

There were no consequences from Young's address. There was no strong support nor were there loud objections. There was silence.

Unions just want the issue to go away. What would be the function of a labor union if the workers owned a significant part of the corporation? We cannot expect active union management to support the concept of worker ownership.

## The Concern of Brandeis

Brandeis was concerned that the ownership of workers would be so small that it would not improve the position of labor. On the other hand, even a small ownership interest might be distracting enough to prevent labor from achieving its reasonable goals.

Brandeis might be correct. But the way to find out is to try the alternative of workers being rewarded with stock ownership. Would it reduce conflict and increase efficiency?

## The Risks

Young gave his HBS talk in 1927. Soon 1929–1932 hit and it was not obvious that common stock was a good investment. Common stocks have risk. In 1932, labor was not likely to accept common stock rather than cash.

Carnegie suggested protecting labor against the risk of value decline. But one of the most important lessons of finance is that common stock ownership has risk and for large stock holdings, there is currently no effective protection against major value declines. It is important for labor to fully understand that the investors in the common stock are exposed to major risks of value decline.

## Restricted Stock?

The stock awarded to managers is often restricted stock, that is, it cannot be sold for a given time period.

Should the stock given (or sold) to workers likewise be restricted? This is an issue that deserves to be debated. All things being equal, I would favor freedom to sell on the part of the owner of the stock. But I do understand the position that the stock should be held by the workers since that is the objective of the stock ownership program.

## Conclusions

In 1911 and 1914, Andrew Carnegie advocated worker ownership of corporations and Owen D. Young reinforced the idea in 1927. These were two of the great American capitalists that give the idea validity. With Carnegie and Young supporting the idea, isn't the idea worthy of consideration? Would ownership affect efficiency and innovations of the workforce? Would the amount of conflicts between labor and management be reduced? It is worth a try.

# Chapter 8

# Correcting One Problem: Introducing Present Value Depreciation

It is normal accounting practice to use either straight-line or accelerated depreciation in measuring a firm's income. We will first consider a situation where straight-line depreciation gives good results and then a situation where the accounting results are not acceptable. The objective of this chapter is to make a manager more sensitive to the fact that a problem exists when an asset has a life longer than one year.

Assume an investment with a 0.15 internal rate of return is accepted with the following expected cash flows:

| Time | Cash Flow |
|------|-----------|
| 0 | −3,000 |
| 1 | +1,450 |
| 2 | +1,300 |
| 3 | +1,150 |

Using straight-line depreciation expense, we obtain the following operating results:

| Period | Cash Flow | Depreciation | Income | Beginning Investment | ROI |
|--------|-----------|--------------|--------|----------------------|-----|
| 1 | 1,450 | 1,000 | 450 | 3,000 | 0.15 |
| 2 | 1,300 | 1,000 | 300 | 2,000 | 0.15 |
| 3 | 1,150 | 1,000 | 150 | 1,000 | 0.15 |

The return on investment of each year is equal to the investment's internal rate of return. This happy result occurs in this situation if straight-line depreciation is used and:

1. The cash flow decreases each year
2. The amount of the decrease is the same each year
3. The amount of the decrease is equal to the depreciation expense times the internal rate of return (equal to 0.15).

Any other sequence of cash flows will lead to distortions. For example, if the positive cash flows are constant, straight-line depreciation expense leads to the early years earning less than the investment's internal rate of return and the later years earning more.

## An Example: Constant Benefits

Assume a firm requires that to be accepted, an investment must expect to earn a 0.15 internal rate of return. An investment with a 0.15 internal rate of return has the following set of cash flows:

| Time | Cash Flow |
|------|-----------|
| 0    | −2,283    |
| 1    | 1,000     |
| 2    | 1,000     |
| 3    | 1,000     |

We will use present value concepts to develop a method of depreciation that leads to a constant ROI each period. We will use the internal rate of return to compute the present value at different moments in time.

Define $V_i$ to be the value of the investment at time $i$. At time 0, using 0.15 as the discount rate, the value is $2,283 and $V_0 = \$2,283$. At time one, we have $V_1 = \$1,626$:

| Time | Cash Flow | Present Value Factor to Bring Cash Flow to Time One | Present Value |
|------|-----------|-----------------------------------------------------|---------------|
| 2 | 1,000 | 0.86957 | 870 |
| 3 | 1,000 | 0.75614 | 756 |
| | | | $V_1 = 1,626$ |

The value at time two based for the cash flow projection is:

$$V_2 = \frac{\$1,000}{1.15} = \$870.$$

The investment's value at time three is expected to be zero.

We will define the depreciation expense of a period to be the change in value taking place during the period:

$D_1 = V_0 - V_1 = 2,283 - 1,626 = 657$
$D_2 = V_1 - V_2 = 1,626 - 870 = 756$
$D_3 = V_2 - V_3 = 870 - 0 = 870$

The depreciation measures that result from this calculation are the "present value depreciation" or "economic depreciation" for the asset. The expected incomes and the ROI's for the three years are:

## Using Present Value Depreciation

|  | Revenue | Economic Depreciation | Expected Income | Investment | Expected ROI |
|---|---|---|---|---|---|
| 1 | 1,000 | 657 | 343 | 2,283 | 0.15 |
| 2 | 1,000 | 756 | 244 | 1,626 | 0.15 |
| 3 | 1,000 | 870 | 130 | 870 | 0.15 |

Note that using present value depreciation, the expected ROI of each period is equal to the investment's internal rate of return.

If we were to use straight-line depreciation expense, the investment is expected to earn less than the required return in the first period and more than the required return in the third period.

## Using Straight-Line Depreciation

|  | Revenue | Straight-Line Depreciation | Expected Income | Investment | Expected ROI |
|---|---|---|---|---|---|
| 1 | 1,000 | 761 | 239 | 2,283 | 0.105 |
| 2 | 1,000 | 761 | 239 | 1,522 | 0.157 |
| 3 | 1,000 | 761 | 239 | 761 | 0.314 |

When the benefits are constant, the use of straight-line depreciation expense results in the early years of life having expected ROI's that are lower than the investment's internal rate of return. These measures of bad performance in the early years may be sufficient to keep the investment from being accepted if managers responsible for the asset are not willing to accept the expected bad measures of performance for the early years of life.

## Another Example: Increasing Benefits

We will now illustrate a situation where the expected benefits increase through time. The distortions introduced by using straight-line depreciation are larger now than when the benefits were assumed to be constant. Assume an investment has the following expected cash flows:

| Time | Expected Cash Flow |
|------|--------------------|
| 0 | −3,000 |
| 1 | 1,150 |
| 2 | 1,322.50 |
| 3 | 1,520.875 |

The investment has a 0.15 internal rate of return. Using straight-line depreciation expense we obtain:

## Using Straight-Line Depreciation

| Period | Cash Flow | Straight-Line Depreciation | Expected Income | Investment | Expected ROI |
|--------|-----------|----------------------------|-----------------|------------|--------------|
| 1 | 1,150 | 1,000 | 150 | 3,000 | 0.05 |
| 2 | 1,322.50 | 1,000 | 322.50 | 2,000 | 0.16 |
| 3 | 1,520.875 | 1,000 | 520.875 | 1,000 | 0.52 |

The expected incomes of the early years are harmed and the later years benefited by the straight-line depreciation method.

Now we will use present value depreciation. We have the following values for $V_i$:

$$V_0 = \$3,000$$

$$V_1 = \frac{\$1,322.50}{1.15} + \frac{\$1,520.875}{1.15^2} = \$2,300$$

$$V_2 = \frac{\$1,520.875}{1.15} = \$1,322.50$$

$$V_3 = 0$$

The depreciation expenses using the above value measures are:

$$D_1 = \$3,000 - \$2,300 = \$700$$
$$D_2 = \$2,300 - \$1,322.50 = \$977.50$$
$$D_3 = \$1,322.50 - \$0 = \$1,322.50$$

The expected incomes and ROI's of each period will be:

## Using Present Value Depreciation

| Period | Cash Flow | Present Value Depreciation | Expected Income | Beginning Investment | Expected ROI |
|--------|-----------|-----------|-----------|-----------|-----------|
| 1 | 1,150 | 700 | 450 | 3,000 | 0.15 |
| 2 | 1,322.50 | 977.50 | 345 | 2,300 | 0.15 |
| 3 | 1,520.875 | 1,322.50 | 198.375 | 1,322.50 | 0.15 |

Using the present value depreciation method, we again have the ROI of each year equal to the investment's internal rate of return. The fact that the benefits are delayed does not adversely affect the ROI of the early years if present value depreciation is used.

Present value depreciation method effectively solves one major problem associated with the conventional use of ROI. It eliminates the commonly found bias against the investment's early years that is present when the straight-line depreciation method or any accelerated depreciation method is used and the investment's cash flows are either constant or increasing through time.

## Units of Production

Present value accounting is new and different. Most managers when first confronted with present value accounting are a bit apprehensive. However, they are comfortable with the unit of production method of accounting.

Usually, the unit of production method is implemented based on the period's actual units of production. To be consistent with present value accounting the procedure could be implemented using the units of production expected for a given period.

A choice between the two methods will depend on whether depreciation takes place only because of usage (in which case the actual production is relevant) or if there is technological obsolescence threatening to shorten the life (in which case the expected production is not relevant).

We will present the example based on expected production, but actual production could just as well be used.

Assume the net revenue of a product is expected to increase from $1.10 per unit at 0.10 per year. The units of sales and total revenues are expected to be:

| Period | Units | Net Revenue | Total Net Revenue |
|--------|-------|-------------|-------------------|
| 1 | 500 | 1.10 | 550 |
| 2 | 1,000 | 1.21 | 1,210 |
| 3 | 2,000 | 1.331 | 2,662 |

The value of the asset at different moments in time is:

| Time | Cash Flow | PV at Time 0 | PV at Time 1 | PV at Time 2 | PV at Time 3 |
|------|-----------|--------------|--------------|--------------|--------------|
| 1 | 550 | 500 | | | |
| 2 | 1,210 | 1,000 | 1,100 | | |
| 3 | 2,662 | 2,000 | 2,200 | 2,420 | 0 |
| | | $V_0 = 3,500$ | $V_1 = 3,300$ | $V_2 = 2,420$ | 0 |

The present value depreciation for each period is:

$$\text{Depreciation of Period } 1 = 3,500 - 3,300 = 200$$
$$\text{Depreciation of Period } 2 = 3,300 - 2,420 = 880$$
$$\text{Depreciation of Period } 3 = 2,420 - 0 = 2,420$$

The incomes and ROI's resulting from the use of present value depreciation are:

| Period | Cash Flow | Present Value Depreciation | Expected Income | Beginning Investment | Expected ROI |
|--------|-----------|---------------------------|-----------------|---------------------|--------------|
| 1 | 550 | 200 | 350 | 3,500 | 0.10 |
| 2 | 1,210 | 880 | 330 | 3,300 | 0.10 |
| 3 | 2,662 | 2,420 | 242 | 2,420 | 0.10 |

Now let us use the production method of allocating the $3,500 of cost. There will be 3,500 units and the cost per unit is $1. The depreciation of each period is:

| Period | Units | Cost Per Unit | Depreciation |
|--------|-------|---------------|--------------|
| 1 | 500 | $1 | 500 |
| 2 | 1,000 | $1 | 1,000 |
| 3 | 2,000 | $1 | 2,000 |

The incomes and ROI's will be:

| Period | Cash Flow | Production Basis Depreciation | Income | Beginning Investment | ROI |
|--------|-----------|-------------------------------|--------|---------------------|------|
| 1 | 550 | 500 | 50 | 3,500 | 0.014 |
| 2 | 1,210 | 1,000 | 210 | 3,000 | 0.105 |
| 3 | 2,662 | 2,000 | 662 | 2,000 | 0.331 |

The results are not as good as using present value depreciation, but they are better than using straight-line depreciation (better in the sense of being closer to showing a constant ROI of 0.10 per year and

not showing an operating loss in any year). The straight-line depreciation and ROI's of each year are:

| Period | Cash Flow | Straight-Line Depreciation | Income | Beginning Investment | ROI |
|--------|-----------|---------------------------|--------|---------------------|-----|
| 1 | 550 | 1,167 | −617 | 3,500 | Negative |
| 2 | 1,210 | 1,167 | 43 | 2,334 | 0.018 |
| 3 | 2,662 | 1,167 | 1,495 | 1,167 | 1.28 |

While the units of production accounting method is not as good
as present value depreciation, it is likely to be better than the results
of using straight-line depreciation or some method of accelerated
depreciation.

We could further improve the production basis of computing
depreciation by taking into consideration the timing of the units
produced and sold by a time discounting process. We have not taken
that step since it introduces a complexity and with that degree of
complexity, why not use present value depreciation?

In determining the units to be used in computing the units of
production with a capacity increasing investment, one has to be
careful to include the units of output resulting from the investment.
Assuming some increase in efficiency, there will be units shifted
from old production units to the new investment. If the primary
motivating factor was the added capacity and not the added efficiency, basing the depreciation on total units produced (including
the shifts from other units) would overstate the depreciation of the
early years.

This complexity can be bypassed by the use of present value
depreciation.

**Negative Depreciation**

Assume $10,000 is expended at time zero to earn $12,100 at time
two. This is an 0.10 internal rate of return. The value of the asset at
time one is $11,000.

If the income and the ROI of the first time period is computed, we find the present value depreciation is a negative $1,000 leading to $1,000 of income and a ROI of $\frac{1,000}{10,000} = 0.10$. This negative depreciation jolts many executives. It occurs because the asset becomes more valuable as the time of the large positive cash flows comes closer. We are not accustomed to depreciation expense being negative, but there is no logical reason why we should not expect an asset to increase in value rather than decrease over part of its life.

### Gaming by Management

Unfortunately, even as fine a tool as present value depreciation has its deficiencies. One problem is that management in presenting an investment proposal can "back load" the project. The cash flows of the early years are estimated to be low and the cash flows of the later years are set high so that the investment is acceptable, but the necessity of doing well is relatively far in the future.

The solution to gaming a project is for top management to review the plan associated with the investment and determine its acceptability. Is it reasonable for the expected cash flows of the early years to be set at low values? If it is reasonable, then the targets being set may be sensible.

### Using the Gross Investment

Consider the following investment costing $3,000 with an internal rate of return of 0.20.

| Period | Cash Flows | Straight-Line Depreciation | Income | Beginning Investment | ROI |
|--------|-----------|-----------|--------|-----------|------|
| 1 | 1,600 | 1,000 | 600 | 3,000 | 0.20 |
| 2 | 1,400 | 1,000 | 400 | 2,000 | 0.20 |
| 3 | 1,200 | 1,000 | 200 | 1,000 | 0.20 |

Now we will shift to the use of gross investment rather than the asset's depreciated cost. Assume the analyst does not trust the accuracy of the depreciation accounting.

| Period | Cash Flows | Straight-Line Depreciation | Income | Gross Investment | ROI |
|--------|-----------|----------------------------|--------|------------------|------|
| 1 | 1,600 | 1,000 | 600 | 3,000 | 0.200 |
| 2 | 1,400 | 1,000 | 400 | 3,000 | 0.133 |
| 3 | 1,200 | 1,000 | 200 | 3,000 | 0.067 |

In year one, the firm earns an ROI equal to the internal rate of return, but in both of the other two years, the ROI is less than the asset's internal rate of return.

The use of gross investments to measure performance will result in management implicitly raising the return required for finding investments to be acceptable. If the firm (top management) thinks a 0.20 return is required, operating managers will require an investment to earn more than 0.20 to be acceptable so that 0.20 is more likely to be earned.

If the required return is 0.20, the above investment will be rejected if gross investment is used for the accounting. This result occurs if a management is concerned with its apparent performance since it fails to meet that return on investment requirement in two of the three years of its life.

## Cash Flow ROI

Another way of avoiding the complications of depreciation calculations that have been advocated by some practitioners is to use a cash flow return on investment. Since cash flow is used to evaluate investments it would seem to be logical to use it to measure performance. Unfortunately, it does not work out to be a correct method for performance measurement or for computing incentive compensation.

Consider the above investment that costs $3,000 which has a 0.20 internal rate of return. Using the cash flow ROI and straight-line depreciation, we obtain:

| Period | Cash Flow | Beginning Investment | Cash Flow ROI |
|--------|-----------|----------------------|---------------|
| 1 | 1,600 | 3,000 | 0.533 |
| 2 | 1,400 | 2,000 | 0.700 |
| 3 | 1,200 | 1,000 | 1.200 |

Note that the cash flow ROI is much larger than either the 0.20 internal rate of return or the 0.20 ROI's using the incomes. The use of the cash flows in computing the ROI will result in measures that are not at all related to the asset's internal rate of return. A manager would find it very difficult to use the cash flow ROI measures intelligently (effectively).

## Conclusions

Present value depreciation expense is not widely used in practice. While its advantages in theory are easy to illustrate, in practice, management frequently does not want to initiate a third accounting system (the financial accounting and tax accounting are already in place).

Some day present value depreciation accounting will be at least as generally accepted as straight-line depreciation. In the meantime, management frequently has the choice of using it or subjectively adjusting for the distortions caused by straight-line depreciation expense when the benefits from the investment are constant or increasing through time. One cannot automatically accept forecasted or actual accounting results without analyzing the effects of the accounting practices on the income measures.

# Chapter 9

# Using Earnings Per Share and Stock Prices to Measure Managerial Performance

Investors tend to be disappointed when the earnings per share (EPS) goes up and the stock price goes down. In this chapter, we want to consider critically the use of EPS and stock price as performance measures.

### Earnings Per Share

Is an increase in EPS desirable? All things equal, an increase in EPS is a desirable event for which management should be praised. However, it is possible to have an increase in EPS that does not reflect good managerial performance.

Consider an increase in EPS that arises because of an accounting change, or results because of manipulating the current accounting rules. This type of increase in EPS is of low quality, and management should not receive special awards or praise because of its performance. For example, a firm can increase its current income by decreasing research and development expenditures. But future incomes are likely to be penalized by the absence of new products.

Another way of increasing EPS is by changing the financial structure. If the firm is earning a higher return on capital than the after tax cost of debt, a substitution of debt for common stock will increase the EPS of that year. Without other information, we cannot conclude that a change of this type is desirable and even with the information we may be uncertain about our conclusion. The increase in the amount of debt might be desirable but the increase in risk must be recognized.

EPS can also be increased by merger activity. If a firm with a price earnings multiplier of twenty to one acquires a firm with a price earnings multiplier of ten to one, the EPS will increase for that year. Again, we cannot be sure that the move is desirable. The growth rate of the firm with a twenty to one price earnings multiple is likely to be decreased by the acquisition.

While all of the above reasons cast doubt on the routine use of EPS as a performance measure, the most significant objection is that the EPS measure is computed without considering the cost of the capital used and the firm's capital structure. Any retention of earnings in a project that makes some income will increase EPS but it might not be a desirable action.

Assume a firm with 1,000,000 shares outstanding is earning $2,000,000 per year or $2 per share. It has a capital cost of 0.15. It invests (retains) the $2,000,000 and earns an additional $100,000 (assume this is a perpetuity). The new EPS is $\frac{\$2,100,000}{1,000,000} = \$2.10$ and EPS has increased from $2. But the increase was the result of accepting an investment with an ROI of 0.05 when the firm's capital cost has been defined to be 0.15. The investment that caused the EPS increase was not desirable.

The EPS calculation to be used for performance measurement would be improved if we used an economic income measure applied to the capital being used. It is desirable to reflect the opportunity cost of the capital being used. As conventionally used, EPS is a very approximate measure of performance that lacks the preciseness needed to measure performance for a management incentive plan consistent with the firm making optimum decisions. A firm's competitive position is not improved by making bad investment decisions.

## Stock Price

One problem with using the stock price as a measure of performance is that the stock price and performance can move in different directions. A firm might do well in a time period where the stock market in general is doing badly. The general market fall can drag down the price of the firm doing well.

A second problem is that a division may be doing outstandingly well but the firm may be doing poorly. When there is a divergence between the performance of the several divisions, it is difficult to reward everyone fairly on one basis.

But let us assume that the use of stock price as the basis of incentive compensation is restricted to those managers directly and clearly responsible for the firm's overall operations. Even now there are complexities. Assume that the plan was for the firm to earn $4 per share and management did so well the earnings were $5 per share. Unfortunately, the stock price of $40 at the beginning of the year went to $20 at the end of the year despite the increase in earnings.

There are many possible explanations why this strange event can happen. One is that while the actual earnings of $5 exceeded the planned earnings of $4, the market expected the earnings to be $8 per share thus was disappointed with the results.

A second explanation is that the cost of money went up. When the earnings were $4, assume the dividends were $2 and the market expected a 0.10 annual growth. With a 0.15 required market return using a conventional valuation model we would have:

$$\text{Price} = \frac{\$2}{0.15 - 0.10} = \$40$$

where the $2 is the expected dividend, the 0.15 the cost of equity capital, and the 0.10 is the growth rate in dividends.

When the earnings are $5, we could have the cost of equity increase to 0.20 and if the growth rate stays at 0.10, we will have:

$$\text{Price} = \frac{\$2}{0.20 - 0.10} = \$20.$$

We could also have a change in the market's expectation as to the firm's growth and this would also affect the firm's stock market price.

If we used a more complex valuation model, we could also vary elements of risk and cause a stock price change because of different risk perceptions.

A final difficulty with using the stock price is analogous with one of the objections to using the firm's EPS. Stock price can be increased in an absolute sense by making investments that are not as desirable as they should be. Thus, a firm might retain $20,000,000 and this amount could be invested in assets with a present value of $15,000,000. The NPV of the investment is a negative $5,000,000 but the effect on the value of the firm's stock equity is to increase it by $15,000,000 compared to the payment of a dividend. Now it could be that the position of the stockholders would have been enhanced by a distribution of the $20,000,000 to them. Thus, the increase in stock value, by itself, is not a sufficient measure of the firm's financial performance.

In general terms, we can be in favor of increases in both EPS and stock price. Such increases are likely to be desirable. But it is extremely difficult to use these measures as the basis of a management compensation plan or to judge the profitability of the corporation without modifying the conventional measures to cope with the types of complexities described in this chapter.

Any stock option plan is a method of rewarding management for stock price increases, and is subjected to the limitations described above. We should try to give management the type of incentives that lead to decisions that would be the decisions that an informed group of shareholders would make if they were making the decisions directly.

## Short Run–Long Run

Corporate managements are frequently accused of excessively focusing on the short run effects of decisions. How will a decision affect the next quarter's earnings and today's (or tomorrow's) stock price?

There would seem to be some justification for the concern. In fact, there is justification for management to pay consideration to the short run. There is little satisfaction in knowing that you made the right decision, if it was the reason why you got fired.

A president of a major one product corporation engineered the acquisition of a firm that was actually larger than his firm and that gave his firm access to world markets. The board of directors was warned that the acquisition would temporarily depress earnings per share but that in the long run the new growth rate would more than compensate for the temporary depression.

Unfortunately, the forecasted negative effect on EPS was accentuated by a severe business recession, and within six months of the acquisition, the president was fired (interestingly, he was replaced by the president of the acquired firm).

Another complexity is the fact that the accounting measures (income and ROI) tend to be very hard on the firm's performance in the early years of a new asset's life. If this institutional effect is reinforced by the fact that the investment starts up slowly (low cash flows in the early years), we have a lot of incentive for an insecure management to reject the investment.

All good investment theories say that the entire life of an investment is important, not the accounting measures of the early years. In fact, good investment criteria leave out the accounting measures of income and ROI. But in the real world these pro-forma measures are computed and form a major hurdle to having investments accepted. The present value method of depreciation would go a long way to solving the problem, but this solution is not widely applied, and will not be applied more widely for a long time.

When a large percentage of the salary of an executive, and maybe even the job itself, is tied to the next quarter's and the next year's earnings, it would be surprising if management did not consider how the next decision would affect these short-term earnings.

## A Solution: Use the Long Term

One solution to the problem of short-term focus for managerial financial compensation is to use a longer period, say, three, four, or five years, as the basis of financial awards.

Assume a corporation evaluates Mr. Jones over a three-year period and he has 12 months to go (24 months have transpired). A long-term decision now becomes the short-term decision. The decisions of the next 12 months do not affect the past 36-month measures. The effects of the decisions in the next 12 months become very short term.

To solve the above problem, the results of any given year are not conclusive until the results of $n$ future years are factored into the analysis. Assume a manager earns $100,000,000 and a return of 0.15. Both are very good performance achievement. But suppose in the next year there is a loss of $250,000,000 and in year 3 there is a loss of $300,000,000. The $100,000,000 of income gets wiped out and the manager's performance gets graded to be unacceptable. The consequences of decisions made today should be considered tomorrow.

Given the on-going nature of business, we must use a multi-year block of future years as the basis of measuring performance. For practical reasons, what will happen in the years following this given block are not considered. The system must be practical.

## Conclusions

It is very easy to list some performance measures that are intuitively appealing and enhance a firm's competitive position and should be included as inputs. These include:

EPS
Market price
ROI (and the spread between the ROI and the cost of equity)
Growth in earnings and assets

But none of these measures can be used without care and fear. They can all give managers incentives to make less than optimum decisions. Knowing the potential weaknesses of these simple, but wrong, measures is an early step towards improving performance and performance measures, thus improving competitiveness of the firm.

# Chapter 10

# Ten Management Errors

Knowing and understanding the problems of achieving an optimum competitive position is the first step to finding the solution. In this chapter, there are listed ten practices called "management errors". These are often encountered faulty practices that lead to a high likelihood of less than optimum operating decisions and lead to increasing the likelihood that the firm will cause itself to become less competitive. They are all correctible. Some of these practices can be defended because under some conditions, they work and while some of the practices are intuitively appealing, they also tend to tempt management to make incorrect decisions.

**Error Number 1:** Have short-run pro-forma accounting information affect real decisions.

A decision should be made based on the economic consequences of the decision over its life. Accounting measures are the result of convention and they focus on relatively short time periods. This combination means that the short-run measures of income and return on investment are not reliable bases on which to rest long-run decisions.

Management should be educated as to the very limited usefulness for decision-making of the conventional pro-forma accounting information.

**Error Number 2:** Tell managers of strategic business units to maximize return on investment (ROI) and reward the managers accordingly.

A maximization of ROI can lead to the divestment of economically desirable units. At the extreme, if the objective is to earn the highest ROI feasible, only the unit earning the maximum ROI would be retained.

The focus on increasing the ROI also leads to the rejection of investments that have ROI's that are above the minimum required return but earn less in the project's early years than the ROI that is currently being required. Top management frequently does not learn of those projects that are not submitted.

Finally, this error can lead to a focus on the short-run ROI effects rather than the change in value that will take place over the asset's entire life.

**Error Number 3:**  Top management tells operating management to maximize a combination of ROI and growth.

This decision criterion is in the correct direction. Using a growth factor combined with ROI eliminates several of the problems arising from just using ROI.

However, implementing this criterion correctly is very difficult. We have to decide on a ranking of different combinations of ROI and growth. It is likely that the ranking will create situations where undertaking undesirable investments may lead to a higher ranked combination of ROI and growth.

If the use of economic income were declared unusable, then the next best choice would be the use of ROI combined with a growth measure, but the use of NPV for investment decisions would dominate the alternative methods of analysis.

**Error Number 4:**  Tell management to maximize EPS or the stock price.

All things equal, the higher the EPS and the larger the stock price the better. Unfortunately, there are strategies that can be used to increase these measures which decrease the economic well-being of the common stockholders. All things are not necessarily equal.

If economic income and ROI and growth are currently being used, then EPS and stock price would be the next most attractive measures.

**Error Number 5:** Use a historical long-term cost of money for determining the cost of using working capital if the short-term cost of money is greatly different.

We want decisions affecting the amount of working capital that is being used to be sensitive to the current cost of money. This implies that each unit be charged, using the current cost of short-term money, for the magnitude of the working capital that is currently being used by the unit.

It is crucial that working capital decisions be affected by the current costs of money. With long-lived assets, it is more important that the interest cost be well defined and predictable. For long-lived investments, a reasonable measure to use is the capital cost at the time of making the investment. For working capital, the current short-term rate for obtaining capital should be used.

**Error Number 6:** Divest "non-profitable" units.

It is reasonable to divest units where the present value of the cash flows obtained from divestment exceeds the present value of the cash flows from operating the units. Whether or not the units are "profitable" or the ROI is not "satisfactory" is not relevant. The conventional ROI is computed using sunk costs to measure the investment and this measure is not relevant in deciding whether or not to divest.

When deciding to divest or not, a comparison of present values is useful. An analysis of current profitability is not useful except to provide warning signs (e.g., as a forecast of future earnings).

**Error Number 7:** Starve divisions for lack of capital if they do not qualify based on the classification resulting from the firm's corporate strategy.

Classifying units by their growth prospects and then using different required returns based on these classifications is likely to lead to faulty decisions.

It is understandable that if a division's unit sales are decreasing in a shrinking market that plans to expand capacity will not be looked at favorably. But what manager would submit expansion plans with these conditions of decreasing sales?

But even a division with no or little unit growth possibility might still require and deserve the opportunity to spend capital for cost-reduction projects. In fact, if enough corporations follow the strategy of starving their units for capital, a unit with efficient equipment might experience a sales growth despite the fact that the overall market is not growing.

Conclusion: Each investment should be considered on its own merits (net present value) and it is possible to have "good" proposals from "bad" divisions. Setting higher hurdle rates based on the origin of the proposal is not useful. This policy merely accelerates the destruction of a unit that could conceivably be viable. It can rapidly convert potential cash cows into loss dogs. Even cows should be fed capital if the facts indicate that the investments are desirable and competitive on a profitability basis with other proposals.

**Error Number 8:**  Require the same return for all assets of a division.

Different assets of the same division can have different risk. There is no reason why all assets of a division should be treated the same relative to risk adjustments. We can have a safe investment with a risky division and a risky investment with a safe division.

Another risk problem is where a manager is willing to undertake very risky (not desirable) investments in order to make a reputation (if the investment is successful). The other extreme is where a manager will only undertake very safe investments because of a desire to keep on the same career path with little probability of being bumped off because of an investment mistake leading to a loss.

**Error Number 9:**  Require the same return for all divisions.

One way or another, investors want to be compensated for risk. If the risk of an investment is large, the return expected to be earned should also be large.

This implies that divisions with more risk should also be expected to earn larger returns through time.

Given that a division can be risky (thus a higher return is required) but an investment within that division can still be relatively safe, we want a procedure that can easily take these risk differences into consideration. The economic income procedure does so effectively and simply.

**Error Number 10:**   Do not charge for capital (it's only an allocation), or do not charge a fair (economic) amount.

We have been critical of a wide range of different measures of performance and methods of basing a managerial bonus incentive plan. We should not neglect to be critical of those plans that do not charge for the capital being used. This error ranks high in the list of errors that should be avoided.

The use of capital has a cost. It has a cost whether the capital is debt or common stock, whether it is new capital or retained earnings. Management should be charged a fair amount for the use of this capital.

One can find cases where debt capital costs 0.14 but management is being charged 0.05 for the capital being used. Any return over 0.05 increases management's bonus pool.

If all the capital were acquired when capital cost 0.05, a utilization of this rate would be acceptable (but not for working capital). But more likely the 0.05 is a holdover from a long past period and it has not been updated. Management has no incentive to increase the percentage since the increase would reduce the bonus pool.

There are two problems that have to be solved. One is determining the total pool of bonus money to be made available to management. Second, determining how the pool is to be allocated among the managers. To solve either of these problems, we need a good measure of the cost(s) of the capital that is being used.

## Conclusions

We conclude that economic income is a major tool for measuring income and for designing managerial incentive plans. It is flexible (different capital costs can be used for different assets), theoretically correct, and easy to use and understand. It is likely to be consistent with the application of the NPV method of making investment decisions.

Some persons will argue that managers will make the correct decisions despite the misleading incentives of ROI. It is not important whether they are correct or not. The likelihood is present for there to be a lack of congruence between the actions of the operations manager and the goals of the corporation. Since the divergence of decisions and goals can be easily rectified by a sensible performance measurement scheme, we do not have to determine whether managers are susceptible to being moved by financial rewards to make less than optimum decisions from the stockholders' viewpoint.

We can refine the economic income measure by using sophisticated depreciation methods and by the use of current bid prices for assets rather than the historical sunk costs, but these are bell and whistle types of refinements. They are less important than the use of economic income.

The prime virtue of economic income is that it benefits a manager to recommend the acceptance of desirable investments (this statement is completely correct if present value depreciation is used, and partially correct otherwise). The consistency of the decision process and the performance measurement-compensation plan is essential. We cannot expect a manager to make decisions that benefit a firm if those decisions adversely affect the take-home pay of the executive.

One final recommendation is appropriate. Use basic theory and logic and not labels and fancy names. The economic income concept is attractive because it is effective and leads to desirable decisions. The name is mundane. It would never sell on Madison Avenue. But consider "Value Leverage Index" or "Value Creation" or "Shareholder Wealth Creation". These terms take wing right into our hearts and minds.

While we would not want to reject a concept just because it had an attractive name, we also should not be influenced by the name in choosing between different practices. The strengths and weaknesses of each approach should be the basis of the choice, not the promise of its name.

There are those who are critical of rational management. But are they favoring irrational management? No. They are really against wrong-headed analysis and analysis that is too complex to be useful and too unwielding to be flexible. We should agree with this analysis, but still be in favor of right-headed rational analysis.

I argue in favor of theory and rational decision-making, but a rational decision-making that does not exclude the consideration of qualitative factors.

Economic income is a valuable managerial tool. But Alfred P. Sloan said it best[1]:

> An essential aspect of our management philosophy is the factual approach to business judgment. The final act of business judgment is of course intuitive. (Sloan, p. XXIII)

and

> The figures did not give automatic answers to problems. They simply exposed the facts with which to judge whether the divisions were operating in line with expectations as reflected in prior performance or in their budgets. (Sloan, p. 142)

Sloan's book is worth reading.

---

[1] Alfred P. Sloan (1963). *My Years with General Motors.* Doubleday and Company, Inc., New York.

# Chapter 11

# Costs of Capital by Division

It is important that capital be allocated to the divisions that promise the best mix of return and risk. Different divisions have different expected returns and different risks. Should not each division have its own cost of capital? Unfortunately, the business world is even more complex than this. Not only do different divisions have different risks but different assets within a division are likely to have different risks.

Let us put aside the question of whether the risk should be defined by the division in which the asset is located or by the basic nature of the asset. Assume that for any asset with more risk, a larger return is required.

Define $r_f$ to be the default-free return (the return on a federal government security). The required return is increased as risk is increased. At zero risk, an investment only has to earn a return equal to $r_f$. As the amount of risk increases, the return of the asset of the division has to earn increases also.

If we have a multi-period investment, then we have problems combining the risk adjustment and the time-value factor in one measure called the discount rate. This is not an exact science. Assume a risky investment is said to require a 0.25 return and a very safe investment can be acceptable even though it only earns 0.10. But these simple ways of defining the required returns may not be sufficient tools for coping with investments with different amounts of risky cash flows extending over many time periods.

## The Risk Measure

As risk increases, the required return also increases. Some finance executives would prefer that we be more specific in defining risk. One possibility offered by finance theory is to use the Capital Asset Pricing Model and define risk in terms of an asset's Beta, or systematic risk. That is, the risk of an asset is only related to how its return is affected by changes in the overall market return. If the asset's return is expected to go down by 20 percent when the market's return goes by 10 percent, we would describe the asset as being very risky. If the asset's return is expected not to change if the market's return changes in any way, the asset would be described as being riskless. Most managers would say this is not an adequate description of risk.

If we were to define risk purely in Capital Asset Pricing Model terms, all risks except for the systematic risk would be ignored in determining the asset's required return. A product requiring an investment of $100,000,000 with a 0.5 probability of being declared illegal in its first year, would be described as having zero risk if the sales and profits of the product are not correlated at all with the return one earns on a market basket of securities. Most managers and investors reject the theory of ignoring all risks other than market risks. Management is not perfectly diversified. Thus, we return to a more general, all-inclusive definition of risk.

If an asset has more risk, it is necessary to expect a higher return if the asset is to be acceptable. The acceptance of this premise is a long way from then concluding that all investments made by a risky division should promise a higher return or be rejected. Some investments made by a risky division will be safe investments, thus will not require a risk premium.

Let us assume that a firm defines the minimum return that it would accept for a riskless investment to be 0.08 but that on the average for Division B (a risky division) it requires a 0.15 return.

With a 0.15 target return the division's management would have a strong incentive to reject any investment with an internal rate of return that is less than 0.15. But even a risky division can have safe investments so a strict application of this policy is not a desirable policy from the overall viewpoint of the firm.

Again, the economic income approach comes to our rescue. Assume a riskless asset costing $1,000 promises a return of 0.10 (the firm only requires 0.08 for a riskless asset) at time one. The income statement for the asset would be:

| | |
|---|---:|
| Revenue | $1,100 |
| Depreciation | 1,000 |
| Income before interest | 100 |
| Interest (0.08) | 80 |
| Economic Income | 20 |

The asset contributes $20 to the division's economic income, thus management has an incentive to accept it if the economic income method is used. If ROI is used, then the fact that the division must earn 0.15 on the average might lead to a rejection of this desirable investment.

## Classification of Divisions

A well used managerial fad was to give a label to a division. Thus divisions were labeled:

Expansionary
Emphasis
Sustain
Selective

If the return required by a division depends on the label that is attached to the division, then we must be careful that the required return will achieve the desired objectives.

Thus, we could have the following requirements for cost reduction investments:

| | |
|---|---|
| Expansionary | 0.15 |
| Emphasis | 0.20 |
| Sustain | 0.30 |
| Selective | 0.40 |

These rates were taken (with minor adjustments) from the capital budgeting manual of a Fortune 500 firm. This practice was actually used.

Note that the "Selective" divisions have to earn a 0.40 internal rate of return to accept a cost reduction investment (they cannot make a capacity expansion investment in any circumstances). The use of such a high hurdle rate (required return) guarantees the fact that the division will rapidly be unable to compete. Management's incentive in the "Selective" divisions is to look for another job since the "Selective" divisions are doomed. The "Sustain" divisions are not quite as badly off, but they can expect to slip into the "Selective" classification shortly since their competitive position is also likely to be eroded.

With cut-off rates of 0.30 and 0.40, the method of evaluating performance becomes a relatively secondary type of issue. The allocation of resource decision has replaced it in importance. The method used to allocate capital will determine the ability of the firm to compete.

## How High a Hurdle?

There are some who argue that if the cost of capital is 0.12, the required return should be higher than 0.12 because there are nondiscretionary projects that use capital but do not generate cash flows (these projects may be dictated by government). Thus, they want a division to reject investments below the current average ROI.

Assume a firm's capital cost is 0.12, and there are two divisions, one earning 0.15 and the second earning 0.30. Do we want the division earning 0.30 to reject investments between 0.15 and 0.30? Do we want the division earning 0.15 to reject investments that earn more than 0.12 and less than 0.15? Consider the following investment with the cash flows being certain:

| Time 0 | Time 1 | Internal Rate of Return | Net Present Value |
|--------|--------|-------------------------|-------------------|
| −1,000 | 1,140  | 0.14                    | $18               |

If the investment is accepted the firm will have more cash at time one to pay for other capital that may be needed than if the investment is rejected. As long as the investment earns more than the required return (sensibly set) the firm will be better off with the investment.

If the investment causes other capital expenditures to be made, then this fact should affect the cash flows, and thus affect the investment's return on investment and NPV.

## Conclusions

There is a reasonable desire on the part of a firm's top management to simplify decision-making by making an easily applied set of rules or classifying assets so that decisions are more or less automatic.

Requiring that divisions earn returns consistent with their average risk is a reasonable desire. But the fact is that applying rules that all investments must earn the same minimum return can lead to bad decisions. The economic income performance measure with different capital costs for different risk levels helps us to bypass one complexity. However, the classification of divisions so that some divisions are starved for capital introduces another dimension into the managerial incentive systems. Managers who see their divisions labeled for not receiving capital have a strong incentive to look for another job.

Managerial decision-making is a complex process. Attempts to simplify by broad classification and excessively high discount rates are likely to lead to less than optimum decisions. With a 0.40 discount rate, a $100 received in twenty years is worth $0.12 today. Excessively high discount rates make it difficult to accept long-lived investments.

# Chapter 12

# Mergers, Acquisitions and LBOs

The consultant was pleased to hear from one of his favorite firms. The firm had switched to a discounted cash flow investment evaluation procedure many years ago and had excellent results in developing a sensible capital budgeting methodology. The initial joy turned into chagrin as he discovered the purpose of the call. The firm was involved in defending itself against a raider and as part of the defense there was a financial restructuring. The major component of the restructuring was the increase in the amount of long-term debt from $350,000,000 to $2,000,000,000. As a result of the additional debt (and increased cash flows to equity investors), top management decided that it was necessary to reduce the capital budget for the coming year from $300,000,000 to $120,000,000.

If the company had started with a capital budget loaded with water, the reduction could be welcomed by investors. But our consultant knew there was no water in the budget. In fact, middle management would have argued before the restructuring that a capital budget of $500,000,000 was more appropriate for the firm's investors than $300,000,000. Now the budget was being reduced by $180,000,000 to $120,000,000. Our consultant was given the charge of developing a systematic approach to capital budgeting when there were $500,000,000 of acceptable projects and only $120,000,000 were to be accepted. In addition, the debt is going to require massive amounts of immediate cash outlays, thus, accepted investments will have to generate large cash flows in the early years of life.

An analogous position arises when management is concerned about the short-term earnings per share and accepts and rejects investments in order to maintain the short-term EPS goals. All of these factors tend to distort a firm's investment decisions and its ability to compete in the global markets.

The above example illustrates a corporate restructuring situation where the implication is that the society is harmed by the shrinking investment outlays. The same type of situation can also take place with a merger, acquisition, and a leveraged buyout (LBO). But, to be fair, we should also consider the positive effects of these transactions. Above it was assumed that the firm had $500,000,000 of desirable projects. A cynic could conclude that only $100,000,000 were economically desirable.

Generally, LBO transactions involve the issuance of massive amounts of debt. The debt payment requirements plus the fact that management frequently has a significant ownership percentage imposes fiscal and operating disciplines. There is little or no room for inefficiencies. Management works doubly hard to make sure all monies are spent wisely.

In addition, mergers and acquisitions give the opportunity for management to streamline operations. Duplications are eliminated and society benefits from the more efficient operations. When Chevron acquires Gulf Oil the total employment of the new Chevron is not the sum of the old Chevron and old Gulf corporations. While there are horrendous costs to individuals who are dislocated by the merger, there can be a net efficiency gain to society.

A negative consideration to the merger and acquisition process is that managerial time and effort is spent resisting overtures from unwelcome acquirers. In addition, there are massive amounts paid to investment bankers for first acquiring firms (or defending against acquisitions) and then divesting them a few years later. Firms first go private and then go public with investment bankers being paid for both transactions. The costs of these transactions may be a price that has to be paid for achieving some increase in efficiency, but it is a large cost.

While some mergers and acquisitions arise because inefficiencies exist and can be eliminated by a restructuring, it also appears that a major motivation for firms going private is the exploitation of the economic advantages of debt compared to stock with a tax law that allows interest as a tax deduction but not dividends.

Any thinking management has two choices as it chooses a capital structure. One is to issue a reasonable amount of debt that allows the firm to accept a reasonable amount of risk. Unfortunately, this strategy leaves the firm vulnerable to the acquisition efforts of a person or corporation willing to use a larger amount of debt.

The second choice is to borrow a maximum amount of debt, thus leaving the firm unattractive to any sensible raider. Unfortunately, this strategy often leads to the firm's inability to undertake economically desirable investments and makes the firm vulnerable to a downturn in business activity.

The tax law leads to an unnecessary encouragement of corporate raiding. The tax law is not neutral to the merger process. Earlier, I recommended several changes in the tax law to eliminate these motivations.

## The Motivation to Use Debt

We want to make clear the nature of the tax motivation to use debt.

Assume a situation when debt costs 0.10, the corporate tax rate is 0.35, and a corporate is paying income taxes of $100,000,000 on taxable income of $285,700,000. This earning and tax situation will continue into the future.

The objective is to maximize the flow of cash to the capital contributors. By substituting $2,857,000,000 of 0.10 debt for common stock, there would be $285,700,000 of interest, zero taxable income, and zero income tax. Each year the investors (now debt holders) would be better off by $100,000,000, the amount of taxes saved. Using the 0.10 debt rate as a discount rate, the value of using debt instead of common stock is $1,000,000,000 or equivalently:

$$\$0.35(\$2,857,000,000) = \$1,000,000,000.$$

The tax motivation for a corporation with taxable income to use debt is very large, if the stockholders are making the capital structure decision.

## The Return on Investment Illusion

The use of debt creates the potential for increasing the return on the stock equity capital. Assume a $1,000 investment with a life of one year promises an IRR of 0.20. For simplicity, initially assume the tax rate is zero.

| Time 0 | Time 1 | |
|--------|--------|--|
| −1,000 | +1,200 | 0.20 IRR |

Assume that 0.20 is not large enough to attract investors. The promoters borrow $800 of 0.10 debt. The cash flows are now:

| | Time 0 | Time 1 | IRR |
|--|--------|--------|-----|
| Basic Investment | −1,000 | +1,200 | 0.20 |
| Debt | +800 | −880 | 0.10 |
| Net to Equity | −200 | 320 | 1.60 or 160 percent |

The equity investment now is expected to earn 160 percent. This trick only requires that the cost of debt be smaller than the basic investment's IRR and a willingness by the firm to use debt.

The improvement in return is somewhat of an illusion that is revealed if we explicitly make the investment's cash flow risky. The risk to the equity investors is increased by the substitution of $800 of debt for equity.

To make the example more consistent with actual practice, assume a 0.35 corporate tax. With no debt, we have:

| Time 0 | Time 1 | IRR |
|--------|--------|-----|
| Basic Investment | −1,000 | +1,200 | 0.20 |
| Tax | | −75 | |
| Net to Equity | −1,000 | 1,125 | 0.125 |

Now, again assume $800 of debt is used.

|  | Time 0 | Time 1 | IRR |
|---|---|---|---|
| Basic Investment | −1,000 | +1,200 | 0.20 |
| Debt | +800 | −880 | 0.10 |
| Net Before Tax | −200 | 320 | |
| Tax | | −42 | |
| Net After Tax | −200 | 278 | 1.39 or 139 percent |

The IRR on the equity investment is increased from 0.125 with zero debt (and a 0.35 tax) to 139 percent with $800 of 0.10 debt.

The use of debt is powerful both to reduce taxes (the tax in the example is reduced from $75 to $42) and to inflate the return on equity capital (increased from 0.125 to 1.39 or 12.5 percent to 139 percent).

## Greenmail

The prime example of a counter-productive activity is greenmail. It occupies management's time, and if successfully executed, results in one group of stockholders being treated preferentially compared to other stockholders.

The first step in the greenmail process is for a raider with a very negative reputation (a reputation for dismembering corporations and firing the present management) to obtain a significant ownership position in a firm, and indicate a desire to take control of the firm.

The second step is for the firm's management to set forth a restructuring plan which includes a buyout of the raider's position. Usually, this buyout is a favorable arrangement relative to what the other shareholders will be offered.

The primary opposition to the above process is based on the fact that the raider receives more per share than the other shareholders. This is not fair. A secondary factor is that for some period of time (one to three months), the firm's management thinks of little except the defense against the raider.

One reasonable solution is for corporations to include in their charter a fairness provision that insures all shareholders be given the same opportunity to sell their shares at a given price.

A second solution is for the courts to decide that it is not legal for a corporation to show preferential treatment to a select group of investors.

A third solution is to pass a set of new laws that would be aimed at preventing greenmail. This was done in the United States by imposing a tax penalty on the firm paying greenmail.

The problem now is that there is the potential for new legislation that could be aimed at making it more difficult to acquire a firm thus helping entrenched inefficient markets. An acceptable law would be one which insured that all shareholders were treated fairly by the corporation in a situation when the corporation is buying shares.

## Conclusion

The corporate restructurings, LBOs and mergers and acquisitions are heavily influenced by the current tax laws and there is need for an elimination of the tax motivation (see Chapter 2). On the positive side is the fact that the corporate capital structure changes can lead to increased efficiency. On the negative side is the reduction in the amount of risk a firm can accept after the addition of massive amounts of debt, as well as the costs imposed on the firm being attacked by the raiders.

Economic efficiency would be served by the proposed change in the tax law that eliminates the tax advantage of debt. But aside from an appropriate tax law change and elimination of greenmail (requiring at a minimum changes in corporate policies or charters), there is no reason to legislate against merger, acquisition and LBO activity. The potential improvements in efficiency outweigh the costs that are incurred.

Managements can become greedy and lazy. The threat of a takeover by another firm or by private equity firms can force a firm's management to achieve levels of efficiency not previously feasible and thus increase a firm's global competitiveness.

# Chapter 13

# Little Differences and Big Results

Society must be careful in analyzing the effects of its actions. A small change in economic incentives can have a large effect on output. The wrong change can lead to the destruction of a firm's competitive position.

Those of a conservative bent tend to think that the present situation is to be preferred over radical change. However, it is necessary to question whether there are not desirable changes that have little cost and large benefits. In this chapter, we will explore a few areas where change might well be desirable.

### Government Spending, Deficits and Productivity

There is a tendency to focus on the federal deficit as having great significance, as indeed it does. But even more important than the size of the deficit is the general level of Federal Government spending (as a percentage of the GNP) and the nature of the spending.

A large part of Government spending is a form of consumption. There are, of course, many examples of government investment (roads, dams, bridges, airports, etc.) but the largest amount of Federal Government expenditures is a form of consumption. Social Security and Medicare (more generally, health expenditures) are two examples.

The fact is that with full employment any Government expenditures bids away resources that would otherwise be invested or consumed directly in the private sector. With less than full employment it is possible that the Government spending will result in a larger sum of production (GNP) than if the Government had left it to the private sector to consume. But we are concerned here with the situation where the Government spending competes with the private sector for scarce resources. Engineers and scientists working on Star Wars are not working on a better automobile, air transport, or plumbing system.

Wars are terrible events and all rational people want to avoid them. Many countries spend enormous sums to maintain the peace. In the past, wars have been fought for economic gains (sources of raw material or markets or more land). Now a different type of conflict exists where the winner does not gain economic victories, but incurs enormous costs.

There are legitimate economic and social reasons for Government expenditures to take place, but the fact is that when the Government spending is more than society can afford, it contributes to the foreign trade deficit. In addition, non-investment type of Government spending reduces the ability of the economy to invest in productivity improvements.

## The Sale of Expertise to Competitors

There are many ways of selling expertise. At one extreme is giving it away and at the other extreme is having it stolen. In the middle are the explicit sales of economic expertise.

This is a difficult section because there are so many different parties and different objectives. We can approach this issue from the viewpoint of the world community and be happy whenever information of any type is communicated from one sector to another. We will take a more provincial viewpoint and will primarily consider the consequences from a specific national economy.

## Outsourcing

During the 1980s and the years following, "outsourcing" became a very popular technique. It refers to the purchasing or manufacturing of components or finished goods in a foreign country. The motivation was to reduce costs.

In the middle of the 1980s, an hour of manufacturing labor cost approximately $15 in the U.S., $9 in Japan, $2 in Korea and less than a $1 in the People's Republic of China (CRP). The U.S. firm would set up its own firm in a country such as the above or contract with a foreign firm or the government, and teach that entity how to produce the product needed in the quality and quantity needed.

The immediate result of successful outsourcing by U.S. firms is reduced costs and less manufacturing jobs in the U.S. The long-term result is less easy to predict but it is clear that the U.S. firm having stopped manufacturing the part is off the learning curve. It is very difficult to return to the manufacturing process once it has left since the other producer now has both know-how and lower labor costs.

In addition, the U.S. firm is apt to fall behind in product design since it is more difficult to know the optimum mix of design for manufacturing and use. Thus, outsourcing, which seems like the ideal solution for enabling the U.S.-based firm to compete in the presence of high U.S. labor costs, has many long-term costs that should not be ignored. Outsourcing is one solution to a difficult problem, but it should not be the only solution that is used. There are many advantages to having the source of parts close to the assembly operation.

## The Sale of Technology

Not too many years ago when technology was sold overseas, it was good technology but old and inferior to the new technology that was available.

Now technology is frequently transmitted via a joint venture endeavor and the technology is apt to be newer and better than that contained in the U.S. plants. Again, short-term benefits are sought with little concern for the long-term costs. A future competitor is being helped to catch up on the technology front.

When technology is sold, the foreign purchaser is benefited by the competition among U.S. firms for the sale. As firm believers in the value of competition, we are not clever in our foreign dealings. We frequently export the benefits of competition.

Should U.S. firms be allowed to join forces in order to compete more efficiently (and profitably) in world markets? Remember we could not stop OPEC from raising the price of oil from $2 to $100 per barrel.

My recommendation is that the possibility and desirability forming export trading companies should be studied. These cartels would be supervised to insure that domestic competition would be maintained.

Note that I have not said I am in favor of such cartels. A great deal of study of the costs and benefits would have to be conducted before a conclusion is reached. However, I am sure that a study of how U.S. firms compete overseas is desirable.

## The Business School Dean

Not too many years ago, a United States-based major business school established an MBA program in Asia, staffed with its primary scholars (teachers).

Shortly after starting the program, the Dean of the school was interviewed by a newspaper. The Dean was asked to justify his school's educational program given that it would enhance the ability of the Asian country to compete with the U.S. corporations. The Dean's reply was a classic. "We do not teach anything that will help our competitors".

Now, I will attempt to answer the question for the Dean. Frankly, I do not know what the correct response is, or what it should be, but I know that the given (printed) response was nonsense and I can try to improve on it.

Knowledge and education should be readily available. One function of any educational institution (such as a business school) is to spread knowledge to other countries. Improving the lot of other countries will improve the quality of life in other countries. The fight is against mother nature and not against the people who happen to live in a different geographical area. Thus, the Dean's non-U.S. program is likely to have a beneficial impact on the U.S. citizen's well-being if only to decrease the cost of imports.

Knowledge is important to achieving a good competitive position. It would not be possible to have a normal MBA program without teaching elements that would enhance the competitiveness of a country's industrial firm. But this is good not bad.

## An Anti-Trust Program

The desirability of having high level of competition have been well stated and the laws of the United States are designed to insure competition (there are triple damages assessed against the firm that acts unlawfully to reduce competition).

I have only one point to make regarding the administration of our anti-trust program. It is now necessary to consider the competitors in the world market and not just the U.S. firms. Also, we have to consider how to make U.S. firms more competitive on the international scene. This might lead to allowing (or encouraging) joint ventures that in the past would have been considered to be illegal.

This difference in approach to interpreting the anti-trust laws could make a difference in the ability of U.S. firms to compete profitably in foreign countries.

## Annoying Inefficiencies

Being a rich country, we have been able to afford annoying inefficiencies. Consider the rebate system. One buys some products for $9 but is told that the net cost after a $5 rebate is $4.

This sounds simple enough but consider how the rebate is achieved. The first step is to find a coupon at the store's check-out counter (they are frequently stored in random order). Second, the sales slip must indicate that the item has been purchased. Third, some type of proof has to be detached from the product. The filled-out coupon, sales slip, and evidence must be sent to an address in the far west (or south or north). Don't buy two rebate items at the same time since you would need two sales slips. After two to four months, assuming no errors, you will be sent a check for $5. Probably, you make an error and will receive nothing.

There is the time spent by the purchaser, two mailings, the processing by the rebate firm, a check, the processing of the check through the bank clearing system after cashing by the purchaser.

Value added to the economy? Waste and frustration and anger (for the time and effort and delay in receipt of the check or not receiving anything). Can we really afford such an inefficient mechanism for reducing the price of a product?

Obviously, the objective is to achieve a sale (the $4 price is attractive) and a large number of purchasers will never survive the obstacle course leading to the $5 rebate. Andy Rooney, where are you now that we need you?

A second annoyance is to shop in a grocery store that pays double for product coupons. The customer ahead of you has bought 100 different items and it takes the check-out clerk ten minutes to process the order. It takes the check-out clerk another fifteen minutes to process the 120 different coupons. Is the item for the coupon actually purchased?

Who wins with coupons? How many times are they counted? How much cheating is there? Who pays for all this foolishness?

Someday foreign investors will realize the opportunity to eliminate rebates and coupons and aggressively invade the U.S. retailing industry. Or will they first be pre-empted by these annoying gimmicks?

The coupons and rebates both use resources and are unnecessary devices for reducing prices. Economic theory says that both will be driven from our midst if I am correct and most customers find them to be annoying artifacts. Only time will tell if I am correct. However, our point is somewhat broader than coupons and rebates. A country can no longer afford obvious inefficiencies. If all competitors are using rebates, we have to consider a price reduction as an alternative. If all competitive stores are giving double coupons, we should consider having the lowest prices in town, and not accepting any coupons. Let us end the lemming style of managerial decision-making.

## Conclusions

That which worked well previously may not work well now. It is time to challenge the status quo and look for new solutions. Solutions that are intuitively appealing and reduce waste should replace solutions that include obvious wastage and are undesirable from the viewpoint of society.

Let us be intelligently daring and change that which we cannot defend as being sensible.

# Chapter 14

# Scientific Management

Wouldn't it be nice if management was purely scientific? Well, there is a body of knowledge called scientific management. Frederick Winslow Taylor, born in 1856 (died in 1915), is called the Father of Scientific Management (an efficiency movement).[1] He was a mechanical engineer and an early management consultant who changed the way that hourly workers were evaluated and rewarded. In fact, the actual jobs were frequently revised based on studies conducted using Taylor's theories and practices.

## The Manufacturing Process

Taylor's method was to break down a job into components. Each component would be timed with a stop watch and a standard for the task would be established.

Both the breaking down of tasks and the establishing of standards became normal practices in production shops. Stop watches and clipboards were essential tools of a production floor.

## Louis Brandeis and Taylor

Louis Brandeis was first a very liberal lawyer and then a very liberal supreme court justice. He actually introduced the term "scientific

---

[1] For an excellent book length description of Taylor's achievements, see Copley F.B. (1923). *Frederick W. Taylor, Father of Scientific Management*. New York and London: Harper and Brothers Publishers.

management" in 1910 in a case involving the railroads and the Interstate Commerce Commission. The railroads claimed that they could not increase wages without increasing freight rates. Brandeis argued that by using Taylor's scientific management techniques, wages could be increased without increasing freight rates. Of course, Brandeis was interested in increasing wages and not in promoting Taylor's theories.

## The Objections

Taylor's focus on efficiency (especially the presence of the stop watch) soon attracted critics. Taylor neglected to consider the social values in evaluating the work processes. Translating the work to small segments meant there was no room for the worker as an artist or an expert.

But the "Efficiency Movement" of which Taylor was an important leader, was an important factor leading to the great prosperity in the United States during the period 1900–1930. His ideas on manufacturing were also used around the globe (e.g., France and Switzerland).

## The Elements of Scientific Management

There are elements of scientific management that there is agreement about and elements about which there is disagreement. First is the replacement of *ad hoc* methods with methods of production that result from system study of the tasks being undertaken. Equally important, is the education and training, by the corporation, of carefully chosen qualified employees. Each worker then receives instruction and supervision that enables the worker to do the job better.

The final step involves the evaluation of the worker's performance as he/she does the job.

The primary criticisms of Taylor's methods are in the designing of the job context of the worker's activities and the rigid standards that are established (again, time and motion studies and the stop watch). The Taylor methods provoked several strikes and numerous complaints by workers of the rigid nature of the job designed by Taylor's methods.

Taylor was accused of being obsessed with efficiency. Work, with Taylor, became monotonous and skill was absent, not being necessary.

## Others Who Advocated

Carl Barth was an early consultant on scientific management and later in his career, taught at the Harvard Business School.

Lillian Gilbreth introduced elements of psychology to scientific management. Frank Gilbreth (Lillian's husband) helped apply new and better techniques of time and motion studies.

Both Harvard and Dartmouth business schools devoted a significant percentage of their MBA programs to Taylor's scientific management.

## Henry R. Towne

It is important to recognize the contributions of Henry R. Towne to the early development of scientific management. Consider the following statement of Towne.[2]

> To ensure the best results, the organization of productive labor must be directed and controlled by persons having not only good executive ability, and possessing the practical familiarity of a mechanic or engineer with the goods produced and the processes employed, but having also, and equally, a practical knowledge of how to observe, record, analyze, and compare essential facts in relation to wages, supplies, expense accounts, and all else that enters into or affects the economy of production and the cost of the product.

Towne encouraged the writing and publication of papers dealing with the management of production.[3]

> Essentially it was a plea for the recognition and the organization of "the Science of Management"; the plea being based on that principle

---

[2] Ibid., pp. 399.
[3] Ibid., pp. 399–400.

of the higher cooperation for which Taylor came so firmly to stand; namely, that it is not permissible for men to go on repeating their experiences and experiments, that they should take advantage of one another's.

## Conclusions

Frederick Winston Taylor was one of the early pioneers who tried to introduce system into management by introducing well thought out practices into the management of production processes. While Taylor is called the Father of Scientific Management, he can also be called one of the fathers of management education. He was an early professor of management at the Tuck School of Management at Dartmouth and the Harvard Business School relied heavily on Taylor's work in its MBA program.

While one might not want to apply a pure Taylor approach of time and motion studies to a modern production line, there are elements of Taylor's production methods that all modern manufacturing firms would want to apply in their effort to be world competitive.

# Chapter 15

# Corporate Strategies

There are remaining pieces to be filled in the puzzle of how a firm can achieve an improved competitive position. We can define all these pieces to be aspects of corporate strategy.

### Best Practices

A corporation may be doing the best it can in all aspects of its business but there is one additional thing that must be done. Are competitors doing it better? Searching out the best practice for all aspects of its business and then implementing the best practice is a necessity. A program of best practice implementation is a necessity to be competitive.

### Choice of Production Location

Where on the globe should the firm's production activities (broadly defined) be carried on? One company considers the educational level of prospective employees to be the most important factor. Another considers the hourly cost of labor. The list of factors that might be considered is long. Obviously, the choice of location is important and will greatly affect the firm's long-term competitive position.

### The Annual Planning Cycle

Assume each division of the firm must annually present its operating plans and strategies for the coming twelve months to the firm's top management. Included in the presentation are the divisions' forecasted income, revenues, and expenses. There should also be defined the most likely risk to the forecast and what can be done to avoid adverse consequences. The primary objective is, to the extent possible, to avoid top management having unpleasant surprises.

## Outside Help

There are times when a product line of a firm does not offer growth opportunities and firm's management team is out of ideas. At such a time, the acquisition of a corporation with a product line that fits with the firm's product line or to acquire a management that would add valuable skills and knowledge. Acquisitions can add growth and efficiency potential. A reasonable (well thought out) acquisition strategy can help keep the firm competitive.

## Technology Leadership

Just as a country needs a quality educational system if it is to compete effectively in the world economies, a company must be at the cutting edge of technology if it is going to hold on to its market share and grow. Knight and Dyer make this and other important points in their book, *Performance Without Compromise*.[1]

One method of gaining technology is via one or more acquisitions of competitive firms. This can be achieved if the technology will be more valuable if used by the acquiring firm compared to it being used by the firm being acquired.

## Exiting a Business

There comes a time when a business should be exited. One option is to shut the activity down. This alternative has few positives. There might be some salvage values and some tax loss deductions, but essentially there is zero or near zero positive cash flows. However, negative flows might be eliminated.

---

[1] Charles F. Knight with Davis Dyer (2005). *Performance Without Compromise*. Boston, MA: Harvard Business School Press.

A second alternative is to sell the activity. If the cash flows from selling exceed the present value of the cash flows from operations, then this is a signal for the firm to sell.

A third possibility is when the unit is making positive cash flows, but does not fit the corporation's plans for the future. No desirable offers to buy have been made for the unit. A commonly used solution is to give the ownership to the firm's stockholders. This can be done in one of three ways. One is to form a separate corporation and give common stock in this new corporation to the parent's shareholders (this is called a spin-off). A second solution is to sell shares in this new corporation in the market (the remaining shares can be given to the parent's shareholders). Done correctly, the issuance of the shares of the parent's shareholders can be tax free. This is called a carve-out. The third method is a split-off. The shares of the new corporations can be obtained in exchange for shares in the parent. This transaction can also be tax free.

## Managing Mistakes

A very good baseball player will, on the average, get three hits out of ten at bats. Seven times out of ten he/she will fail. However, a couple of the seven failures may have been well hit balls that did not happen to fall in the right spot. The same is true in business. Sometimes, a right decision will turn out badly. Sometimes, a bad decision will turn out so that it looks good. Management must look beyond the numbers that give an obvious result that may not have sufficient explanatory power.

It is desirable that management be patient with bad decisions that are a surprise. Firstly, a firm wants its managers to take reasonable risks that offer the potential for good returns. This means that for all decisions there will be some probability of a bad outcome. Secondly, even the best decisions have some probability of bad outcomes. You do not want to fire a manager for a good decision that turns out badly.

If the original analysis that will lead to a decision to undertake the project was faulty, then the process should not be acceptable as presented.

## Conclusions

The term "corporate strategy" means different things to different people. In this chapter, the term applies to different practices, frequently taking place at corporate headquarters that affect the direction that the firm takes.

Decisions are made and then implemented by people. The effectiveness of a corporation and its ability to compete depends on how the top management makes decisions and then implements the corporate decision process.

It is traditionally assumed that financial incentives lead to improved decision-making at the managerial level. Thus, managers are given the opportunity to own the firm's common stock. They may be given the stock at zero cost or a discount from the market value. In this book, I argue that if stock ownership is desirable, from the corporation's viewpoint, for managers, it is also likely to be desirable for lower levels of employees, such as hourly employees.

# Chapter 16

# Achieving an Improved Competitive Position

This book focuses on a few select issues regarding the objective of improving the competitive position of a firm. There are many areas that need expansion. For example, to improve the relations with hourly employees, it is suggested that the percentage of employees encouraged to own stock be increased. The ownership of stock is likely to increase the harmony of the workforce and the firm and increase the firm's efficiency. But obviously, there are many other steps that can be taken by management to achieve the same goals.

## Improved Financial Reporting

A manager listened to the lecture that explained that an economically desirable investment might lead to several years of not acceptable results, despite achieving the forecasted cash flows, because of the conventional accounting (straight-line depreciation accounting). Told that he had to be patient, he responded that he could be patient but his boss would not be, and he would be fired if he followed the recommended policy.

The basic choice in motivating management and hourly workers is frequently thought to be "the carrot or the stick". A variation of this is the choice between theory X and theory Y (choosing between a very authoritarian system of punishing failure or a more flexible system of encouraging success). This book says nothing substantive about these classic issues. Rather, the objective of this book is to offer a framework for developing a measurement strategy for rewarding employees in a fair manner that supplies the maximum incentive for making decisions that optimizes the well-being of the firm and its shareholders.

The concepts of this book are of most interest to any entity where a manager is responsible both for the magnitude of the operating income and the amount of assets used to earn that income. We are dealing with "profit centers" that use assets, thus are "investment centers".

The consequences of using conventional accounting to measure managerial performance are likely to lead to incentives to reject good investments that would improve the firm's competitive position. To have good investments accepted by a firm, the top management must see beyond conventional accounting.

### Improved Financial Decision Processes

There is general agreement that the NPV method of analyzing investment alternatives is superior to the alternative methods of analysis. But too often other methods are used and the NPV conclusions are mistakenly set aside.

Consider the fact that many firms use the expected ROI (return on investment) of an investment to evaluate its desirability. The IRR (internal rate of return) effectively takes into account the timing of the investment's cash flows. The ROI does not, therefore the ROI measure cannot be used with confidence as the sole measure to evaluate investment opportunities.

In a competitive economic world, no firm can afford to use inferior methods of analyzing investment alternatives. A workforce with inferior tools is not going to be effectively competitive no matter how well-motivated and skilled they are.

We want to develop a set of useful numbers on which to base management compensation. We want better ways of determining whether or not management has done a good or bad job. Using conventional measures, a manager doing a good job can have bad performance measures, and a manager doing a bad job can have good performance measures. Equally important, presently used measures can encourage the acceptance of bad investments and the rejection of good investments.

As bad as current practice is, the really disturbing thing is (and the fact motivating the writing of this book) that a wide range of persons are attempting to implement even worse technique and measures.

Consider a worker whose performance today is outstandingly good, but if we evaluate the results of today's decisions in three years, we find that the results of the decisions were horrendously bad. Obviously, we can only evaluate many of today's decisions in the future.

## The Compensation Policy

One objective of a compensation strategy is to be fair to the managers and hourly workers of the firm. A second objective is to motivate the managers to make decisions that are best for the corporation and its shareholders. We want managers to make decisions that are consistent with maximizing the well-being of the shareholders. The methods used to measure performance to reward managers will greatly influence the decisions that are made. The objective is to develop a performance measurement system that will lead managers to make desirable decisions. The problem is that a large number of the systems currently in use will lead to decisions that are likely to be less than optimum.

In this book, we are concerned with decisions made within an operating entity which is employing assets to earn the income. This utilization of assets is important since it is strongly argued that, while income is an extremely important measure, we do not know how the manager is performing unless we know the amount of assets that are being employed in earning the income.

## Setting and Achieving Goals

Top management should set profit and ROI goals for the firm and in conjunction with operating management should set goals for divisions. This will include the setting of dollars of income targets and ROI's to be earned. A large part of this book is devoted to defining improved measures of these goals, so that the achievement of the goals that are set is consistent with the stockholders' wealth position being improved.

Setting goals is one thing. Achieving them is another. The list is surprisingly short of ways for a corporation to achieve its profit and ROI goals. We will put aside the issue of short run versus long run and consider ways of achieving the basic profit goals. They include:

a.  Cost control, cost reduction, increased productivity and quality: elimination of inefficiency
b.  Improved service and better service than the competitors
c.  Product improvement and innovation
d.  Improved employee morale and thus better productivity
e.  Better and perhaps more selling effort
f.  Obtain assistance (preferential treatment) from the Government or obtain Government business
g.  Better planning (utilization of present resources)
h.  Better investment decisions
i.  In some cases, a modification of the capital structure (debt versus common stock, lease versus debt) might affect income and ROI

This book says very little about how to improve profits by operating more efficiently or by changing the marketing strategy. Instead, it deals with how to get operating managers to seek out the best choices via a sensible incentive system.

## Non-Financial Considerations

This book focuses on the financial measures of performance. This is not to imply that other considerations may not be equally important or even more important.

The famous GM managerial bonus plan was designed so the awards committee had maximum flexibility in making its awards so that it could see beyond the numbers. In the words of A.P. Sloan:

> The Bonus Plan established the concept of corporate profit in place of divisional profits, which only incidentally added up to the corporation's net income. Suitably, it provided for bonuses to be paid to employees "who have contributed to its [General Motors'] success

in a special degree by their inventions, ability, industry, loyalty or exceptional service".[1]

What type of factors would you want to consider if you were on the GM awards committee?

What has the division done to maintain product leadership? Are there new products being developed to replace both the maturing products and the products now new, but soon to age? Are the products efficient?

Is work being done on improving productivity (output and quality)? Are the different methods of production being effectively investigated?

Are all levels of the employees happy and their morale high? Are their skills being developed?

Is suitable attention being paid to customer loyalty? Are unit sales growing?

Are social responsibilities as defined by the board of directors being met?

Are safety and pollution standards being satisfied not only to the letter of the law, but also to the spirit of the law?

Is the physical plant being suitably maintained?

The above listing of questions is not complete, but it is a reasonable sample of non-financial considerations that are of interest to top management, and should affect the financial awards of the managers whose performance is being measured.

## Beyond the Firm

The focus of this book has been the firm and the decisions made by the firm's management. Aside from a chapter discussing the tax system, the book has not discussed extensively issues external to the firm, but these issues are also important.

---

[1] Alfred P. Sloan, Jr. (1963). *My Years With General Motors*, Doubleday and Company, Inc., New York.

Consider the country's education system and the effect this has on the quality of the workforce.

A top executive of a U.S. manufacturing corporation explained his corporation's major investment in China as being the result of the fine education received by the average hourly worker. A better educated workforce in a plant results in the potential for a more competitive plant.

A reliable transportation system also facilitates business operations. A safe and law-abiding environment is also highly desirable.

A good work ethic of all employees is also required. One area had the reputation of being excellent until the workers were paid. After the first paycheck, a large percentage of the workers took a holiday until they had exhausted their cash supply. This was not good for productivity.

## Pensions

In the summer of 2010, a major issue facing the U.S. Congress was whether to pass the law that would have the Government bail out under the water corporate pension plans. Let us consider the issue of a corporation promising to pay a given amount of money for the period of a worker's retirement.

There is no way for a corporation to know today if it can make pension payments in the future, especially unknown large payments that will be a surprise. Making promises that cannot be kept is not likely to enhance the financial viability of a corporation. Why is this important to a corporation's goal of maintaining an excellent competitive position? Imagine a corporation making the choice between modernizing its production line or paying its pension liability. Obviously, its competitive position can be affected by the future pension obligation.

What is the alternative for a corporation making promises to pay cash in the future? A corporation should know what it can afford to pay today. It should make well-defined contributions today to a pension plan and the worker should receive the fruits of those payments in the future. Rather than defining what it will pay in the unknown future, the corporation should define the contribution to be made today.

With an adequate-sized pool of investment assets and with an intelligent investment strategy, it is possible to devise an investment plan with 100 percent probability of meeting reasonable contractual obligations. But most pension plans are not 100 percent funded with the result that there is a significant probability that the pension plan obligations will not be met without disrupting the plan to make real investments in production assets. It is desirable that this contingency be avoided.

While the above has been discussed for the corporate sector, this same type of problem exists for governments promising pensions in real terms for its citizens. Governments should help its citizens save for retirement, but should be wary about promising well-defined real flows in the future which may turn out to be difficult or impossible for any country to afford.

## Conclusions

Achieving good productivity is not the result of applying a few rules of management.

But it would not be wise to ignore the fact that steps can be taken to increase the probability of achieving a high level of competitiveness. One company did well by educating its workers to the reality of the worldwide competition that existed for their job. Competition exists for all products, and only the most dedicated workforce using the most economically efficient tools, is likely to survive to work another day.

There are a wide range of problems and issues facing any top management as it evaluates its own performance and the performance of the firm's divisions. Any firm needs a compensation and measuring performance strategy for solving the problems described in this chapter and other problems not yet described. The firms want a procedure that motivates management to make theoretically correct decisions and rewards managers when they make these decisions and execute the decisions successfully. The accepted procedure is likely to be a compromise, but it should be a compromise that comes close to solving as many of the problems as feasible. As Herbert Simon wrote:

> In an important sense, all decision is a matter of compromise.[2]

The solutions offered in this book are easy to understand. After reading this book, you will be able to accept or reject the logic of the arguments offered. Admittedly, some of the ideas may be too "different" to be implemented immediately. But at a minimum, learning about the deficiencies of present practice and possible solutions should lead to changes in behavior that will lead to improved performance.

Here's to better and fairer management.

---

[2] H.A. Simon, *Administrative Behavior*, Third Edition, Free Press, 1976, pp. 6.

# Subject Index

Alfred P. Sloan   25, 26, 95, 129
Andrew Carnegie   62, 63, 69
Annual planning cycle   121
Anti-trust program   113
Asset redeployment   30–33

Best practice implementation   121
Book value   30, 31, 37

Capital asset pricing model   98
Capital gains tax   8, 9
Carl Barth   119
Carve-out   123
Cash flow ROI   81, 82
Cash flows   14, 16, 17, 20, 28,
   29, 31, 32, 37, 38, 43, 45,
   71–73, 75, 76, 80–82, 87, 91,
   97, 100, 101, 103, 106, 122,
   123, 125, 126
Choice of production location   121
Common stock   6, 7, 10, 11, 25,
   30, 50, 68, 69, 83, 90, 93, 105,
   123, 124, 128
Compensation plan   26, 86, 94,
   127
Compensation strategy   23, 127
Corporate income tax   5–9, 11

Debt-equity ratio   8, 10
Debt-interest deduction   8–10
Default-free return   97
Discounted cash flow   2, 13, 14,
   17, 20, 43, 103
Divestments   36
Divisions   21, 23, 25, 26, 30, 35,
   37, 43, 44, 51–53, 56, 85, 91,
   92, 95, 97, 99–101, 121, 127,
   131
Double taxation   6–8

Earnings on debt   6
Earnings on stock   6
Earnings per share   24, 83–85,
   87, 103
Economic income   24, 33, 35–45,
   50–52, 53, 84, 90, 93–95, 99,
   101
Economic value added   36
Elements of scientific management
   118

Flexi wage plan   48, 55, 56, 60

GM Awards Committee   26, 129
GM Bonus plan   25, 26, 40

Government spending   12, 109, 110

Greenmail   107, 108

Gross investment   80, 81

Henry R Towne   119

Internal rate of return   13, 17, 18, 23, 28, 39, 71, 72, 74–76, 79, 80–82, 98, 100, 106, 107, 126

Investment alternatives   13, 126

Knight and Dyer   122

Leveraged buyout   6, 104, 122

Life cycles   21

Louis Brandeis   59, 65, 117

Martin Weitzman   53

Measuring performance   21–24, 26, 29, 88, 131

Mergers and acquisitions   104, 108

Net present value   13–20, 32, 33, 35, 36, 42, 43, 92, 126

Optimum competitive position 89–93

Outsourcing   110, 111

Owen D. Young   66, 67, 69

Pension plan   130, 131

Performance measure   21, 22, 27, 35, 36, 38, 42, 45, 81, 83, 84, 88, 94, 101, 126, 127

Present value accounting   76, 77

Present value depreciation   71, 73–80, 82, 94

Productivity improvements   13, 110

Profit goals   25, 128

Return on investment   22, 23, 27, 28, 35, 72, 81, 89, 101, 106, 126

Sale of technology   111

Selling expertise   110

Spin-off   123

Split-off   123

Stock equity   6, 8, 10, 11, 48, 50, 86, 106

Straight-line depreciation   28, 29, 71, 72, 74–76, 78, 79, 82, 125

Tax evasion   7, 8

Technology leadership   122

The A&P Case   55, 56

Use of debt   10, 11, 105–107

Valuation models   6

Value index   30, 31

William O. Douglas   64–66

Winslow Taylor   117

Zero tax investor   7, 8